Praise for

Everyday Karma

"A great lady with a gift . . . Her power to heal by helping people understand the roots of their physical ailments is without peer."
—HOWARD M. BEZOZA, M.D., president, The Bezoza Center, New York City, and host, *In the 21st Century*

"An amazing therapist . . . She sees both where you've been and where you're going and becomes your ultimate guide to understanding yourself and thereby helping you to evolve spiritually and emotionally."
—MARIN HOPPER, fashion director, *Elle* magazine

"The scope and magnitude, not to mention multitude, of talents and gifts of this woman are simply extraordinary."
—APRIL MASINI, president and CEO, Masini Television and Film Enterprises

"Carmen has a gift that surpasses other psychics'. Her gift for communicating through metaphysical issues is unlike any other I have witnessed. Her insight and clairvoyance are astounding."
—LYNNE WHITE, Channel 2 *Morning Show* (New York City)

"Carmen Harra is a gifted psychic. Most notable was her level of insight . . . to actually see the revelations of her predictions was absolutely incredible, as if she were writing the script before events happened."
—PAMELA D. HAYES, attorney and campaign advisor to Hillary Clinton

CARMEN HARRA, PH.D.

Everyday Karma

BALLANTINE BOOKS

NEW YORK

I WANT TO DEDICATE THIS BOOK TO
THE MEMBERS OF MY FAMILY—

my loving parents, Victor and Alexandrina;
my daughter, Alexandra;
my husband, Virgil;
my sister, Mona;
and last but not least,
my grandfather.

2005 Ballantine Books Trade Paperback Edition

Published in the United States by Ballantine Books, an imprint of The Random House Publishing Group, a division of Random House, Inc., New York.

Ballantine and colophon are registered trademarks of Random House, Inc.

Originally published in hardcover by Ballantine Books, an imprint of The Random House Publishing Group, a division of Random House, Inc., New York, in 2002.

LIBRARY OF CONGRESS CATALOGING-IN-PUBLICATION DATA
Harra, Carmen.
Everyday karma / Carmen Harra.—1st ed.
p.   cm.
ISBN 0-345-45512-6
1. Karma.   I. Title.

BF1045.K37 H37 2002
133.8—dc21
2002071237

Printed in the United States of America

Ballantine Books website address: www.ballantinebooks.com

4   6   8   9   7   5   3

Book design by Mary A. Wirth

When we die
the only thing
we take with us is
our karma.

CONTENTS

ACKNOWLEDGMENTS

The wise are those who control their body
who control their tongue
who control their mind
and give up what is before
give up what is behind
give up what is between
so when you go on the other side of existence
if your mind is free
you will not enter again into birth and decay.
—BUDDHA

I want to express my eternal gratitude to my mother, Alexandrina, and my father, Victor Muresan, for the unique love and support they gave me in this world and from the parallel world and for continuing to be with me all the time. Our karma was good and resolved. I want to thank my grandfather, who was so right about me when he told me twenty years ago that I would write this book. Although I've never met him in this world, I owe so much to him and love him dearly. I also want to express my love to my other grandparents, Maria, Susan, and George.

I'd also like to thank all of those in this life for their incredible support. My daughter, Alexandra, is the love of my life and I thank her for the many lives we spent together before in Atlantis, Egypt, and Spain. I hope that this book can help her learn to resolve her own karma. This book is also for my dear husband, Virgil, whom I adore for his great spirit and for all the lives we had together in Israel, Turkey, and France. I want to express love and admiration and thanks to my sister, Mona, who provided so much inspiration to me my entire life.

I will never be able to give enough thanks to my agent, Janis Vallely—she is such a beautiful soul; she believed in me and has brought so much good into my life. When I found out her name, I knew she was the agent for me! (Janis was the name of the aunt who raised my mother.) I am eternally grateful to Maureen O'Neal, my editor, for giving me the chance to publish this book. She is an angel in my life.

My deepest thanks to Ray Chambers and Deepak Chopra for their enormous support in helping me to express my ideas. I remain thankful to Frances Jones and Cornelia Guest for all of their help. I'd also like to thank Jennifer Grossman, Lynne White, Jill Castilloni, Jane Greer, Pamela Hayes, Avril Lacour, Aurora Andronache, Odessa Bourne, Alison Swain, and Dennis O'Connell for being in my life, and love to my daughters Carmen and Florina and my grandson Anthony.

And to my dear Susan Pepper, how can I thank you enough? You share the same name as the grandmother

I loved so much, who lived to be 102 years old. You have taken my ideas and spun them into gold.

Finally, I want to thank God for all the lessons I've had to learn in trying to seek wisdom in my life and for allowing me to know love, the biggest blessing of all.

EVERYDAY
KARMA

My Gift of Prophecy and Prediction

Even as a little girl growing up in Romania (Transylvania, to be exact), I knew I was different. After a "near-death" experience at age five, I was able to see things others couldn't. My near-death experience opened my perception to a whole different level of being. I had been given the gift of prophecy and prediction. Some people call it intuition, the sixth sense, or being psychic. I personally prefer to call myself a metaphysical intuitive. I take the wisdom I have gained through my gift of sight and help people apply this wisdom to their everyday lives.

Everyone who has had a near-death experience describes the sensation of "going toward the light." In this parallel world there is extraordinary light energy around you, an inexpressibly beautiful light and no negativity, no fighting, nothing but love. It is a perfect, glowing world, filled with dazzling insights and pure truth, the way our Creator meant it to be, and I've never forgotten it or the lessons it taught me. Why, I wondered, wasn't life on Earth like this?

This parallel world, that I call the Invisible World, is just as real as the physical world here on Earth. It is even more real because the people there are souls unencumbered by ego, emotions, and attachment to material things. Without these negative distractions, love, joy, and peace can exist harmoniously. Even as a child, I knew this was a realm of pure energy, and that I would spend my own life guiding people through that doorway, toward the light. This was my special gift.

I want you to forget everything you think you know about psychics. Surrender your prejudices and skepticism and be open to my message. The way I work is different in that I take the knowledge my psychic abilities have provided me and an understanding of how energy works in the Universe, and combine them with a solid understanding of psychology.

While I do make predictions and prophecies, and have a 93 percent accuracy rate, I am wary of anyone who claims to tell clients a piece of information as if it were written in stone, an inevitable fate. While certain things are predetermined, such as the timing of your birth and death, most things in your life are a matter of free will and choice. The choices you make create your destiny. My purpose in writing this book is to help you make better choices by developing a deep sense of self-awareness. Mankind has learned how to travel to the moon, and even to Mars, yet he hasn't succeeded in traveling inward to knowing the Self. Only in knowing ourselves can we make our lives better and make the changes necessary in the world to create a peaceful and hopeful future.

My gift brings me in contact with celebrities, royalty, high-powered executives, doctors and psychologists, and people from all walks of life. But all of them have one thing in common—they have come to me to gain insight into their problems, make better choices, and find purpose in their lives. I often feel as if these individuals are seeking a new kind of therapy, a way to heal karmic wounds and shape a more positive future.

I've spent the past thirty years developing my psychic abilities, studying metaphysics, and learning about the parallel world of the spirit. I've come to realize that my psychic ability, the so-called sixth sense, is the bridge between the Visible and Invisible worlds. I'm a licensed hypnotherapist, an astrologist, numerologist, and expert in the Kabbalah, cosmology, and astrophysiognamy. These are the tools I use to help you learn more about yourself and the universe you live in.

Most of my clients have been in therapy for years and yet they are still unhappy. They turn to me the way a patient using conventional medicine seeks alternatives. Too often they are desperate—they want to know what the future has in store for them; they want to know how to be happy; they want answers. But my "therapy" is not a magic bullet; it is an interactive process. I can't tell you what is going to happen unless you are able to heal old wounds, so you can discover who you really are and what you want from life.

I have worked with people dealing with problems ranging from divorce, heartbreak, the death of a child, family discord, the loss of a job, accidents, substance abuse, heart disease, cancer, domestic violence, financial disaster, and many other difficult situations. I have helped people find their soul mates, change careers and jobs, stop being workaholics and alcoholics, build their dreams, and detect dangerous tumors or health problems early enough to treat them successfully.

My gift of prophecy and prediction gives me insights that can be shared and taught to others in the here and now. As a psychic I can help you pinpoint your issues, your blocks, your secret dreams. I push my clients to make changes by broadening their perception, by opening a doorway so they can see their infinite potential. Through this book you will see yours, too!

The only way to do this is to learn about your own karma, how to recognize it, understand its meaning, and fix it if it's broken. Simply put, karma is the law of cause and effect: what you sow, you will reap. Your life is a process of resolving karmic issues and in doing so you grow and move on. Unresolved karma breeds negative energy, disease, and unhappiness. Many of the things that go wrong in your life, and in the world, are a result of unresolved karma.

With *Everyday Karma*, I will set you on your own path so that you can begin to understand your life's journey and read the signposts ahead which will eventually become more visible, even without the aid of a psychic guide.

In Part I I will share my personal story and the lessons I gained from the Invisible World. In Part II I will show you how to take these lessons and bring them into your day-to-day life in the Visible World. In Part III I present the foundation of this book: my Karmic Resolution Method which takes you through a ten-step process of recognizing your karma, resolving it, and envisioning a new reality for yourself.

Everyday Karma is the culmination of my life's work; it is a way for me to share the lessons I've learned from the Invisible World by bringing them into focus for you in the visible realm. These lessons have everything to do with karma, our daily thoughts and actions, and how they relate to our relationships, health, and life purpose. *Everyday Karma* will help you heal; it will help you create a better life and a state of mind with balance, security, and confidence. It will show you that life is not about how long you live or how much you accumulate, but what you bring to life, your spiritual legacy. It will take you on a journey of self-discovery that will crack your perception wide-open so you will be free to do what we are all meant to do—enjoy and celebrate the precious gift of life!

PART I

ENTERING THE INVISIBLE WORLD:
THE LAND OF SPIRIT
AND LIGHT

CHAPTER ONE

We Don't Die

In my many years as a metaphysical intuitive, people from all walks of life have come to me, each with their own specific question: "Is he the one for me?" "Will the big deal go through?" "Is now the time to invest in the stock market?" "Is this chronic cough anything serious?" When I give them the answers they usually just stare at me in disbelief. I may tell a client about an exciting new job that is coming up but they won't believe it because it's in a completely different field. Or I'll tell them they will meet the man or woman they're going to marry at a party within the next month but they've sworn they'll never get married again. Inevitably, they'll come back some time later and tell me, "Carmen, you'll never believe it but after I saw you I got a call out of the blue for this job interview and I left the retail industry and now I'm working for a magazine" or "Carmen, I know I said I'd never get married again but just as you said, I went to this party and met a man who wasn't my usual type. We fell in love and are getting married next year."

My clients claim that I changed their lives but in actuality all I did was change their perception. I've shown them all the possibilities and it has affected how they perceive their lives.

I've found that every person has his or her own level of perception and it defines what "reality" means to him or her. Your perception becomes your reality. Perception is really nothing more than our ability to become aware of things through our five senses and then process and understand what we've seen, heard, tasted, smelled, or touched. If you think about it, our physical perception is actually very limiting. We go through life collecting life experiences and processing them through a narrow lens. I believe, no, *I know*, that we all have a perception that goes beyond the limitations of the sensory. We all have the ability to see beyond the five senses into a parallel universe that rises above and beyond the senses. When your perception opens up, you can begin to find the answers to your questions.

My own perception of the world completely changed when I was just a little girl, five years old, growing up in Bistrita, a small town in Northern Romania in a part of the country most Americans think of as the home of Count Dracula—Transylvania.

The Invisible World

It was a beautiful summer afternoon so my parents and I, along with several of our neighbors, went to the Somes River near our town to enjoy the sun and have a picnic. Some of the other children and I left the blankets and were playing on the riverbank farther upstream where the water got a little rougher. I'm a curious adult, but I was an even more curious child, and that day I was standing too close to the riverbank's edge, fascinated by the patterns of the water rushing over the logs and rocks. Mesmerized, I wasn't paying attention to my footing, and I stumbled on a loose rock and fell over the bank.

While the other children ran back to get my parents, I was being dragged down by the river's strong current. I didn't know how to swim and felt myself getting pulled under. I was terrified and unable to keep my head above water. I flailed my arms and cried out for my father but that only seemed to make matters worse and I began to lose consciousness. I was surrounded by darkness and then, in an instant, I stopped struggling.

At that very moment, I was transported out of the dark waters to a place of dazzling light, a world that looked very much like the one I had just left but inexplicably different. When I say that, I don't mean there were houses and cars. It was more like a valley, surrounded by rolling hills of green grass. I was no longer in the water, but above it, in a very peaceful place with lots of trees and flowers, beautiful music, and the most illuminating and beautiful light. And best of all, I was no longer struggling and no longer afraid.

There were people there whom I knew, all dressed in similar white robes, like those you see on a priest or a monk. I could see their faces very clearly and recognized them. Each face was different and although I hadn't known any of them in the world I had just left, I felt that I knew them. They were my brothers and sisters—not my actual brothers and sisters who lived with me and my parents—but people who I knew loved me and would keep me safe. I was surrounded by an intense feeling of love and acceptance, of safety and warmth.

In this other world there was no fighting, no yelling, no cuts or scrapes or bruises on my knee, no being afraid of the dark. The people looked happy, it looked like fun and I wanted to stay there!

I wanted to be with these people. And they wanted me to be with them, too—they beckoned to me, gently calling out, "Come here." I took a step toward them and then saw my body below me, in the river and my father frantically pulling me out of the water. Suddenly the beautiful world was gone, and the people were gone and I was on the riverbank, coughing up water and gasping for air with my father's arms around me.

It wasn't until many years later that I would recognize this as a near-death experience. Many people have described and recorded their near-death experiences and they all describe the same thing—going toward the light. When you actually detach from the physical body you see a world that is beyond the physical and you bask in an extraordinary light energy that is in you and outside of you at the same time.

A traumatic event will often open the doors of perception, but for most people they only open when they are in so much danger that they move outside of the physical plane into the other side. When you are in a physically life-threatening situation a door can open in your mind from the conscious to the subconscious. A door opens that takes you from the visible into the invisible.

This parallel world, what I've come to call the Invisible World, is just as real as the physical world where we live here on Earth. It is even more real because the people there are souls unencumbered by ego, emotions, and attachment to material things. These negative distractions don't exist to cause pain, and so love and joy and peace can coexist beautifully.

This world is a place without negativity, without fighting or hatred; there is nothing but love. In the Invisible World we don't have emotions, we don't hate, we don't experience pain, we're at peace with everything so all we can do is love. It is a perfect world, the world the way our Creator meant it to be, and I've never forgotten it or the lessons it taught me.

That day at the river, I left my physical body for a short time and saw a glimpse of the Invisible World. And yet it wasn't my time to go to the other side. I came back. And in retrospect I realize it was, in fact, just the beginning of my mission.

It has become clear to me since that experience that the Invisible World of peace and light is the way we are all meant to live. We are put on Earth in physical form to gain wisdom and evolve toward that perfection. This is something many religions have been saying for thousands of years, but what they have missed is that we aren't put on Earth to suffer; we are put on Earth to evolve. We exist to be happy and to give and receive love. And most of our suffering holds within it great opportunity to learn and create that evolution.

We Don't Die

The most important thing that I learned by seeing the Invisible World was that there is no death. Our physical bodies may stop serving their purpose but our souls never die. They live on in the Invisible World and have the choice to come back into a physical body again. Often souls choose to come back to the Visible World to work out their karma. And a soul will come back for as many lifetimes as is necessary to do this. I'm certainly not the first person to say this, but to know this in the core of my soul, to have witnessed it, is truly incredible! That knowledge will dramatically change the way you live your life. It will change the way you treat people and it will affect the choices you make in life.

I know this knowledge makes me feel connected to every person and living thing that I encounter. This feeling of connection is with me all the time—I know at the core of my being that separateness is an illusion. I see people not based on how they appear physically, whether they are rich or poor, ugly or beautiful, polite or rude; I see them at the level of their souls. When I look at people I can see right into their memories; I know their joys and I know their sufferings and I share in it. I also know that we are all brothers and sisters on the other side and since I know that at our essence we are all love, that's how I treat people—with love.

I hug people; I tell them I love them; I tell them how grateful I am to have them in my life. I do this with everyone, I can't help it! I meet people and I see the love and beauty in them. I see past the physical body and the ego and I have to tell them, even if I've just met them once. Some people are taken aback by this, but not as many as you might think. Most people are desperate to be loved; they're thrilled to be shown and told that they are loved. It's something none of us does enough. We're all love at our core. Yet we live within the limits of our bodies, starving for the very thing we all have an infinite amount of inside us. We're afraid to show the very love that we are. It's truly crazy!

Although we live in the physical world of the five senses, the world we can hear, taste, touch, smell, and see, this is just a small piece of the greater totality. We are limited by the five senses and by our own fears of the death of ourselves and of our loved ones. But there is nothing to fear. The fact is, we are much more than we think we are; there is much more to life than the sensory world. Often what we see as limitations in our lives are illusions imposed upon us by our enslavement to the physical world and our lack of understanding of the world of energy.

As a way to broaden your perception, think about gravity. If you could eliminate gravity you could eliminate the death of the physical body. Gravity is a phenomenon that only exists on the Earth. If we didn't have gravity we would fall right off the Earth and float into outer space. Gravity influences the density in matter, and since our bodies are matter, gravity makes the body deteriorate and age. If you lived in the space between the Earth and the moon for twenty years, you wouldn't age. When you are in space there is no gravity, no aging, and therefore, the body cannot deteriorate and die. If we were all living in space, instead of on the Earth we would have a completely different perception of what life means. We would know firsthand that the death of the physical body is nothing more than an illusion!

Evil Is the Only True Death

The second important thing that I learned from the Invisible World is that the essence of the Universe, the pure state and intention of existence, is for love and peace and good. In the Invisible World evil does not exist. It is purely an aberration of human nature driven by ego and emotion and nurtured by the amnesia we all experience when we live only in the physical body and forget our souls and our true source and purpose. The only true death in our existence is evil and negativity. And this death occurs only in the Visible World.

Evil is darkness, and everything and anything where negative forces obscure the light. Evil is a lack of awareness, confusion, conflict, betrayal, lies, and limi-

> Good is knowledge; evil is ignorance.
>
> Good is action; evil is stagnation.
>
> Good is order, courage, hope, and faith.
>
> Evil is disorder, insecurity, and desperation.
>
> Evil is the absence of the light.
>
> Good is accepting and working toward the light.

tations. Evil is when we disconnect our physical bodies from the eternal light. Every person has to struggle with this feeling of disconnection but we can feel whole again by acknowledging and integrating the wisdom from the Invisible World into our daily lives. Rather than wasting time fearing physical death, we should devote our lives to eliminating negativity and evil, in our own lives and in our world.

Often we don't even recognize evil because we are so far from the light and so used to the human laws of the walking world. The Invisible World is made up of Universal Laws and the more in touch we are with the Universal Laws, the more we can recognize evil. In the light, evil is exposed. And when it's exposed, it can be eliminated.

We Are All Parts of the Greater Whole

My journey to the other side also showed me that we are all interconnected and part of the greater circle of life. None of us can escape the circle of life, which the Buddhists and Hindus call "Samsara" or the "Wheel of Life." Everything in the Universe is made of energy and all this energy is contained within this circle. This circle has no end, and since energy can't be static, it's in constant, perpetual motion. Everything is in motion; everything is constantly transforming; everything is in a constant state of transition. Since we are all energy and energy doesn't die, we all share in this condition of perpetual evolution and transformation.

Since nothing is fixed, and since we know from physics that the energy of one thing affects the energy of the other things around it, everything in this circle depends on everything else. We are all part of this same circle; we are all part of the greater totality; there is no escaping it. We're all part of the same act and art of creation and we are all connected to one another. It is when we forget there is an interdependence among all living creatures that we make mistakes, become susceptible to wrongdoing, and make ourselves miserable.

A Child's Gift

After I came back from the Invisible World I started to have a different perception of the world and of the people around me. My perception exploded wide-open and I was able to see things before they happened. As a matter of fact, I could see the past, the present, and the future all quite clearly, and all at the same time. I started to hear a quiet voice that told me things, told me what was coming next, and I always tried to listen to it. Eventually I would come to realize that this voice was a spirit guide and I would identify its source, but as a child I didn't question where this voice came from and I didn't worry about "being different." Knowing what was going to happen in advance helped me and so I listened.

What happened to me and what happens to everyone who has a near-death experience is that our perception changes. We are all made up of molecules that vibrate and after a near-death experience that vibration is taken to a higher level and perception broadens as though adding a wide-angle lens onto a camera. In my case, I started anticipating things and knowing everything that was going to happen before it happened. I wouldn't label this experience until I was much older, but essentially I was operating beyond linear time.

When my father's father died it was two years after my near-death experience. I was in the first grade, I was sitting at my desk in school when my father showed up in the doorway of the classroom. I looked up at him and said, "You're here to tell me my grandfather died." I was right. My father's father was only sixty years old and hadn't been sick—he just had a cold—but when I saw my father standing there I just knew.

My family didn't understand what was happening to me when I said things and they tended to brush it off as childish fantasies. Don't get me wrong, my parents were nothing but loving and supportive to me, but at that point in all of our lives, my ability to see things was beyond any of our understanding. My parents led a respectable and simple middle-class existence; my father worked at the local bank, and my type of ability was completely foreign to them. Of course having me as a child would change all that.

My maternal grandfather had been a famous poet and the prime minister of Romania in 1938. The family was told he died of pneumonia, and if you read a Romanian history book today it will say the same thing, but my mother knew that the Communists had killed him by putting poison in his cake. They didn't like his politics. My mother's mother had died when my mother was just one year old so she was left an orphan.

My mother just wanted to have a normal life, without looking over her shoulder, and she told no one about her past. She moved to a small, rural town in Northern Romania where she met and married my father. She raised me in a very simple, hardworking, and traditional household. She wanted to blend in like everyone else, to appear normal. But I was anything but a normal child!

When I was in second grade, in 1963, I heard of this man named Nicolae Ceausescu. I remember saying to my father, "Ceausescu is not a good thing for us." I was a child and knew nothing about politics but I knew this man would bring hardship to Romania. He became president in 1967 and remained dictator until 1989. He became crazier and wreaked more havoc on the country with every passing year. Among other things, he mandated that women couldn't use birth control and that they each had to have five children to help with the industrial workforce. Many children ended up being put in orphanages, raised by the state, and horribly neglected. There wasn't enough food. A pediatric AIDS epidemic swept through the country. Under Ceausescu, Romania suffered greatly, a life without basic freedoms.

Many years after I made this prediction to my father, when I was twenty-one, I was invited to sing at one of Ceausescu's receptions. When I met him face-to-face I immediately had an image of him dead, surrounded by a group of people, and there was a lot of snow and blood. Fifteen years after that meeting, he was murdered after the people of Romania had had enough. It was December, it was snowing and he was shot in the head. On television all over the world people saw the people of Romania celebrating over his bleeding body in the snow.

Despite this image, while growing up my predictions were usually limited to my own childhood universe. For example, I knew when my father was going to get a new job; later on I knew when we were going to move to

Cluj, another town in Transylvania; and I knew exactly what our new house would look like, all before it happened.

And I could always anticipate people's physical problems right away. If my mother had a pain in her leg, or if my father had a headache it would be transferred to me and I would feel it.

Around the time I was nine I started to tell my parents that I was going to be a famous singer. I loved to make up songs and sing, and used to sing all the time while I was walking down the street, much to my mother's chagrin! She used to chide me and tell me it was impolite to be singing all the time, but I could not stop singing. It was as if the songs came out of my mouth all on their own. Of course, now I know that artists are all intuitive in their own way. They take the universal and the invisible and give it form and expression in the physical. At that time, however, I made no connection between my obsession with songwriting and singing and my ability to see things that others didn't.

At that time television was a new invention and it was slow in coming to my small town. As soon as it did, my parents went out and bought a small black and white TV. It was such a big deal for us and we were all mesmerized, as you can imagine! The first time we sat down to watch it I told my family I was going to be on television someday soon. I told them I was going to be a famous singer and travel around the world and be on television. After all, that's what my quiet voice was telling me. They all thought this was very funny. They thought, "She's just a kid with a lot of energy and a vivid imagination; what does she know?" This was a very small town, there were just five thousand people, and people didn't leave, people from Bistrita didn't go off and become famous.

That same summer my family and I went on vacation to the Black Sea. The Black Sea was beautiful in the summer and in Romania we went there the way Americans go to Florida. There was a singing contest going on in town and my family and I sat down to watch it. There were a couple of hundred people in the audience and all of the singers in the competition were in their twenties. They were much older than I was, but still I felt compelled to go up there. So I got up out of the audience and went up onstage and said, "I know how to sing." The audience all broke out into laughter at the sight of this gutsy little girl. The man onstage said, "Are you sure you want to sing?" and I said, "Of course" and broke out into an Edith Piaf song. The audience loved it and laughed hysterically at a nine-year-old singing Edith Piaf. When it was over they gave me a piece of paper, like a diploma, that said I'd been in the contest. All of the other competitors received trophies and I was so mad, I knew they were just humoring me. I told them, "I'm going to be a much better singer than anyone on this stage and I'll be famous!"

It all happened very quickly after that. When I was fifteen I entered a singing competition in school and won. I then went on to the regional singing competition and also won. Eventually I made it to the national competition and won that as well. At the national competition, a record producer came up to me and said, "You have a beautiful voice. I'm willing to give you a chance." By the age of sixteen I had cut my first album as a singer.

I would end up making twelve albums. For the next twenty years I would travel all over Europe: Italy, France, England, Germany, Russia, Turkey, Czechoslovakia, and Sweden. I had grown up speaking Romanian, and I studied French and English in school, but when I traveled I found that intuitively I could speak the language in almost every country I went to. I could also sing in fourteen languages. Although I don't speak Greek, I can sing in Greek. In addition to Romanian, I can sing in Greek, Russian, Turkish, Italian, Spanish, Czech, French, German, English, Swedish, Hungarian, Portuguese, and Hebrew. Anyone from any of these countries will think I share their nationality. I have no idea how I do this! My sense is that it is from my memories from previous lives.

With my gift of song and language I toured most of Europe performing onstage, and yes, on television. I appeared on television in almost every country I visited. Nobody in Bistrita could believe it.

We Are Far More Powerful Than We Realize

As my gift developed and I got older, I went off to college to study art and music but I also began to study metaphysics on my own to try to gain an understanding of what had happened to me. I started to read books about the Kabbalah, astrology, and numerology. I began to study the ancient mystics. I studied Eastern Philosophy, Buddhism, and Hinduism. I studied quantum physics. I read books by all the great psychics and masters. I wanted to understand the source of my gift, the reasons for it. I wanted to put my own experiences in a context. I knew that my experiences weren't normal, they were paranormal; they were not taking place in the physical, they were metaphysical. And so I learned all I could about the paranormal and the metaphysical. And I studied the traditional tools of divination to hone my gift and to help to learn about myself, to access information about who I was and to learn how to use what I knew to help others.

There have been many masters and mystics throughout history who have proven that there is a sixth sense and astonished people with their abilities. I am not talking about magicians or illusionists who use smoke and mirrors or computer technology to trick people on television. I am referring to the prophets, soothsayers, fortune tellers, and psychics who have astounded people since the beginning of time. The Bible is full of prophets, including Jesus Christ, who performed miracles that had enough impact to start one of the world's largest religious movements. Nostradamus had the ability to break linear time and foresee five hundred years into the future with uncanny accuracy, predicting World War II and the Holocaust and even naming Adolph Hitler as the cause. Edgar Cayce, perhaps America's first and best known psychic and healer, who lived at the turn of the last century, has thousands of recorded cases of predictions. He was the subject of a biography, *There Is a River*, first published in 1942 that has never gone out of print because his amazing abilities to see into the future continue to astound people even today. In the 1960s, Neem Karoli Baba, possessing powers to perform the physically impossible—such as levitating above the ground, healing disease, and taking LSD and poison without any apparent effects—became a major figure of the American New Age movement. Today people like Sylvia Browne and John Edward appear on television and make predictions and channel those who have passed on. And while Albert Einstein isn't considered a psychic he has perhaps done more than anyone in our recent history to expose how limited our thinking can be and show how potentially broad our perception can be!

There are many, many recorded cases of people demonstrating gifts that go into the sixth sense and beyond—levitation, telekinesis, telepathy, and the ability to move and alter matter. I once sat in a room with an Egyptian master who was able to transport my coat, from my house on the other side of town, into the room where we were in just ten seconds. This sounds fantastic but I'm not making it up. One minute my coat was in my house across town and the next minute it was in the chair next to me. How did he do it? The fact is our own mind energy is much stronger than we think, stronger than density in fact! Think of karate masters who can chop a wooden block a foot deep with their hands. It's not the power of their hands that cut the block in half—it's the power of their minds. Our minds have the power to go beyond the limitations of the physical. The mind can create its own reality, a different reality than we experience through the five senses. We are just beginning to understand what lies beyond what our limited senses can experience.

Through the years I have come to realize more and more that we all have perception beyond the physical and our minds are far more powerful than we can imagine. Every person has their own level of perception, but it is something that can be expanded and broadened through awareness and practice, or as in cases like mine, through a near-death or traumatic experience. Limited perception keeps us in a psychological prison of sorts. By broadening your perception you set yourself free.

I believe that everyone has the ability to broaden their perception. It just depends on what it is you want to know, and whether you're willing to know. Operating beyond linear time scares a lot of people! But I think this information is freely available. Whatever you want to know, you can know. It all depends on how open you are and how willing you are to listen. If you want to know about a person or something in the Universe, that information is available. Personally, I always thought and acted big. I was never afraid of boundaries. I don't believe in limitations. I never did, and as a consequence I've ended up in situations, places, and with people beyond my wildest dreams.

Scientists have acknowledged that we use only 10 percent of our brain. As a species we are evolving and using more and more of our brain's power all the time. Look at the knowledge we've gained and the things we've accomplished in just the past ten years. We've even cracked the human genome! That must've brought us up to at least 11 percent! Evolutionary studies have shown that at one point human beings only used 3 percent of the brain; thousands of years later we used 7 percent of the brain, and now we use 10 percent. Imagine what we could accomplish if we could tap into that other 90 percent!

We are evolving as a species; we are beginning to accept and learn about the invisible forces that rule our lives and we are beginning to understand that there is much more to this life and to ourselves than we ever imagined. We acknowledge that we have more than five senses. But ultimately the sixth sense is nothing more than the bridge between the Visible and Invisible Worlds. It is just a glimpse into the limitless possibilities the other side has to offer. Beyond the sixth sense there is even more, and we are only now beginning to understand it.

Prediction for Prevention

My feeling is that anyone who has this gift or who develops it should use it to help people have better lives, and to help humanity evolve spiritually. One of my favorite parts of having this sixth sense is making predictions that help people and showing them how to make their own—to project their own futures. Being able to break linear time to allow the mind to see ten, fifteen, or fifty years into the past or the future is powerful and fascinating, but if it isn't doing any good, why bother doing it? Why do past life regression work (using tools to find out what happened to you in past lives) and why go to a psychic to try to find what the future holds for you, unless you're going to gain some understanding that will allow you to make positive change?

The same goes for making prophecies about world events. Nostradamus didn't tell us about Hitler and World War II just so we could be prepared and know it would happen. None of these prophecies are inevitable.

He made the prophecies to help educate mankind so that we could foresee the dangers that would present themselves and we could prevent our own destruction.

In the work that I do I believe the same thing—prediction is for prevention. This belief is at the root of all the work I do. In the Bible God told King Solomon, "I can give you whatever you want. What do you want most in the world?" and Solomon replied, "I want wisdom." In asking for wisdom Solomon proved how wise he already was! Wisdom is the most important thing we can gain on this earth and it is the only way to evolve toward the perfection and harmony of the Invisible World. If we do not understand the reasons behind what is happening to us and cannot make wise and enlightened choices about our future, we will remain lost and destroy ourselves. This is true of us as individuals and as a species.

Everyday I see people who, on the surface, have everything: the successful career, the beautiful house, the fancy car, the rich husband or the trophy wife, but they are still miserable. They haven't just turned down the wrong road, they don't even know where the road is! They have what they think is everything it takes to be happy but they still aren't. They can't see that they should be happy just because it's a beautiful day.

The road to joy exists inside of us, not outside of us. The good is revealed through our thoughts and hearts—our mind and our self-knowledge and broad perception—not through pleasuring the physical body or stroking the ego. The more we stay connected to our higher self, to our soul, and remember the lessons of the Invisible World, the happier we will be. There's no way to use the sixth sense if you allow yourself to suffer under the pressure of the physical world, if you are stressed and are trapped in the problems of your everyday life. Being on earth is difficult and creates many challenges for us, which is why it's even more important to stay attuned to our higher selves. Predictions do us no good unless we use them to choose the higher path, to create change if necessary, and to gain wisdom.

To Predict the Future, Examine the Past and Present

We are in the middle of a turning point in the history of humanity, a world based on all types of scientific and technological inventions and discoveries that have made our quality of life better than it has ever been. Our tremendous progress has been a blessing and should cause us to have nothing but optimism for the future. If we look at the past progress we've made we should be able to assume that we will continue to make the same type of advancement in the future.

Despite this, some of us think this is the end of the world. We live among heartbreaking tragedy, ongoing war, negative emotions like fear and hatred, terrible crimes, a loss of morality, children killing children, toxic thinking, and a pervasive feeling of disconnection. No wonder we feel depressed, anxious, lost, afraid, and confused. It can be difficult to hold on to hope. Sometimes it's easier to believe Nostradamus's prophecies that mankind will be wiped off the face of the earth. But as I said, these prophecies are not "written in stone"— prediction is for prevention.

As Americans, we enjoy a great life of cultural and

technological development and a strong economy. Even when our economy is down, we are better off than most other countries. People are asking, "Has America peaked? Is this the end of our potential?" There are plenty of examples in history of other civilizations that have declined after a long period of prosperity. Some of you may say that history has nothing to do with fore-telling events. But that is wrong, very wrong, since there is no future without the past.

Progress, however, is not the enemy, it's the type of advance we've been making that is the problem. When progress builds a deeper wedge in our feeling of being disconnected from our souls and from the Earth and from other human beings, when it becomes a distrac-tion and becomes our purpose, we are heading toward self-destruction. Ultimately, we are here to evolve but not only in the direction of technological and scientific advancement. We are here to evolve spiritually and to create a world that is balanced. The decisions we make today are crucial because they will affect what happens to us in the years to come. The past, the present, and the future are all very closely tied together.

In order to foretell the future we need to understand that a prediction is very similar to a prognosis. A prog-nosis looks at the symptoms of a disease and tells the likelihood of recovery. Once you have a prognosis, you can begin to treat the disease. This is what I mean when I say that the purpose of prediction is prevention. Hav-ing a solid understanding of where we are in the present and how we got here is crucial in making a prediction about the future. If bad habits have hurt our immune system and made us sick, what do we have to change in order to get better, to be stronger? If we take care of ourselves by eating the right foods, getting plenty of rest, and taking our medicine, our prognosis will look much better. So what is the current prognosis and what can we do to make sure we recover?

We evolved by conquering wilderness, overcoming feudalism and slavery; we've blasted into space; we've extended our life span, but we still don't have the key to the mysteries of our existence. We are the only species with a high level of intelligence and yet we continue to kill one another. We don't learn from our mistakes. We still live with negative emotions like hatred, jealousy, fear, and anger. We don't respect life; we don't treat the world well; we don't understand the basic Universal Laws. We may have changed the world outside but we haven't changed the world inside.

Although we are the most intelligent creatures on earth, we seem to have a very limited capacity to understand why we are here, and we are often hopeless when faced with the unpredictable events life puts before us. We don't seem to have the ability to see the stones on the road, the dangers that are making us fall to the ground, but this limited perception of the senses is just an illusion. We are trapped in the material world and it is imperative that we make a shift in our perception, in our understanding that the true value of life is not the material, it is in the soul. Man is not his body; he is not his senses; he is not his ego. He is a soul living temporarily in a body. Only when man begins to think of himself as divine will he begin to act in a way that is divine. When we begin to tap into the divinity within ourselves, we heal our karma and reach toward immortality. The only worry I have for the future is that we aren't passing along the message of our own divinity.

We look to God for our answers; we ask him for help; we ask him to calm our fears; we ask him "Why do bad things happen?" We look upward with hope and ask God for lessons. The only way we will begin to reflect God's lessons and embrace the Universal principles of the Invisible World is if we get rid of our egos and our negative emotions that keep us tied to the ground. We must empty ourselves and be sincere in our desire for knowledge and purity. This shift in consciousness is not an easy process, but when the collective consciousness is altered, a positive future will lie before us.

The truth is this is not the end of the world; it is just the end of the time in the evolution of mankind: the end of the old order and the beginning of a new order. It is the "darkness before the dawn." The era we are transitioning into is an Era of Awareness when everything will be exposed to the light and the forces of darkness will be eliminated. But in order to solve the mysteries of the future we have to solve the mysteries of who we are.

The Coming Era: From "I Believe" to "I Know"

Humanity is currently in a state of transition. We are making a transition from the period of the past two thousand years, the period of "I believe" to the period for the next two thousand years, "I know." This is the age of knowledge; this time will be the Era of Awareness. When we are aware we can make changes, examine, and erase our past mistakes. We are beginning to understand that there is much more to this life and to ourselves than we ever imagined.

The era of "I believe" is one of "I believe in God," "I believe there is more to us than we currently know," "I believe in love," "I believe in something but I don't know what." As we enter the new era of "I know," rather than just *believing* in God, we will come to *know* God. Rather than *believing* in a mind/body connection, we will come to *know* the mind/body connection. Rather than just *believing* in the power of our spirits we will come to *know* the power of our spirits. Humanity is evolving and as a result, each one of us as individuals will also evolve. We are at a crossroads and must be very conscious as we move forward.

Now, more than ever, it is imperative that we evolve to a higher way of thinking because the world is a reflection of either our limitations or our enlightenment. If we do not evolve and use the full power of our minds, we can never direct the world toward the principles of the Invisible World. We have to expand and change the way we think or we will remain trapped in darkness.

The world we live in will no longer be controlled by negative impulses and feelings. As this shift in consciousness takes place, we will all become more sensitive to the subtle change in vibration, and with it will come broader perception and the understanding that we are the result of a spiritual process. As we evolve we will see that we are no longer victims of fate, that we can master our lives, and exist in harmony with the Universe. In this coming era we will come to know love, forgiveness, and enlightenment. The karma we created for ourselves in the past needs healing and forgiveness, and in the new era, we have the opportunity to begin that process.

This new era will bring much more knowledge, and we have seen some of its evidence already in our breakthroughs in science with the genome project. We will have new perceptions and new laws, that will include everything from a new law of gravitation to the discovery of new planets, to a new frequency that is faster than the speed of light. In the years to come, we will begin to understand the genetic code, to understand and find cures for many of our health problems and diseases. We will no longer kill in the name of God. But more important, we will come to know the secrets of the Invisible World and we will come to live by them.

In many ways this book is about celebrating the concept of survival—we survive; we never really die. We are all transforming and evolving and there are mysteries we are just now beginning to understand. It is our mission to explore those mysteries and to gain knowledge. We each have extraordinary power, (not necessarily sensory power because the sensory is about limitations). With sensory power you can see the wall across the room but you can't see beyond it. I want to show you how to see beyond the wall. If you can acknowledge that your soul and mind are extraordinary, you can learn and gain this knowledge and use it to make your life, and our world, better than any of us can imagine.

CHAPTER TWO

Hearing the Messages from Beyond

You don't have to be a psychic in order to hear the wisdom of the Invisible World—although being psychic certainly helps! With practice and awareness it is possible to communicate with the Invisible World and to glean some of its wisdom. The only catch is that you have to be open and willing to listen to what the spirits tell you. Spirit guides and messages from the Invisible World can come to us in many ways. Although many people's first experience with spirits is from going to a medium or psychic, messages from spirit guides can come to you in signs, synchronicities, déjà vu, and dreams. They can also come directly from someone who has passed over to the other side, in symbols, images, or even in a clear speaking voice that only you can hear.

Even before my journey to the Invisible World, I had a glimpse into its wisdom through two powerful messages told to me by a neighbor who projected my future. Often when we receive messages from the Invisible World we won't understand or acknowledge their significance until weeks, months, or even years later. Unless we are fully awake and in tune with ourselves and the world around us, we may receive messages but not know how to use them. As it was in my case this first time, sometimes we are merely too young or not yet ready to hear what we are being told.

"You Are Like Cassandra"

When I was four years old there was an old woman in a wheelchair who lived next door to my parents. Sometimes my mother would go to her house and bring her food or just sit and talk with her. One day I went over there with her and the old woman looked at me and said, "You have gold in your voice." She paused for a minute, nodded her head and said, "And you are like Cassandra." As a four-year-old I was just delighted to have the attention, even though I had no idea what she meant. Despite that, her words left enough of an impression on me that I never forgot them.

That old woman in the wheelchair was actually my first spiritual guide, because she served as a messenger and made two prophecies that were right on target. The first prediction came true as soon as I made my first album. "You have gold in your voice" predicted that I would become a famous and successful singer and indeed I did. The second prediction I didn't understand until I was deep into my metaphysical studies and stumbled upon the story of Cassandra.

Cassandra was a prophet in the Golden Age of Greece and although she predicted many calamities for her fellow Trojans, no one ever believed her. She told the people, "Beware of Greeks bearing gifts" and vehemently protested when they let the Trojan horse into the city. She knew the giant wooden horse, a gift from the Greeks, was full of enemy soldiers. Of course she was right, and once the horse made it inside the city walls the Greeks were able to attack the Trojans and destroy their city. Somehow the old woman knew that I had Cassandra's gift, the gift of prophecy.

As I told you, after my near-death experience that day at the river, I began to hear a guiding voice that provided me with information that sometimes astounded people and sometimes made them think I just had a vivid imagination. All the time that I was traveling around Europe and focusing on my singing career, I continued to hear the same voice guiding me, and I trusted it completely.

I also found that when I met people, I would inexplicably know things about them. There was a constant stream of communication from the other side. I would walk past someone on the street and I would know if they were suffering from a health problem or a broken heart. Just by looking at them I could tap into their energy and tell them accurate information about their lives. Images and words just came pouring in, one after another, and the information would flow without my asking for it. I was compelled to stop people and tell them the things I heard and saw—I just couldn't help myself. I think some people were taken aback—how could I know so much about them!—and others were simply grateful for the acknowledgment and understanding.

At that time I had a dear friend Anda, who was also a singer and a few years older than I. She would often come to me for guidance. One day in March, I noticed that her aura was very dark and I had a very clear understanding that she was going to die soon and I didn't know how to tell her. She was married and had a little girl, and she was very happy, so I told her that in August she would leave and go somewhere else, to a beautiful and different place. I told her she would experience a completely different way of living that would be better. She didn't understand what I was trying to tell her; she kept asking me questions about where she was going and telling me she didn't want to go anywhere else; she liked her life the way it was. For whatever reason, I was the one who was supposed to give her this message but she couldn't understand it. A short while later, she was diagnosed with lung cancer. She died that year on August 15.

I've always known that the soul needs a few months of preparation before it leaves the body. There's a process, and I could only hope that I helped prepare her, at least on a subconscious level. Some time after she died, her spirit did speak to me from the Invisible World to let me know that she was okay. She is grateful to me for trying to give her the message and helping her prepare and I am grateful to her for letting me know she's okay. The circle of our bond became complete—I gave her a message and she in turn, after passing, gave me one as well.

When Anda passed over, the Romanian newspaper printed an article about her that included my prediction. But even before that, word of my gift got around, and the chorus girls and people I worked with on the road started to line up outside my dressing room for readings and advice. When I was singing in Bucharest, in a place that's the equivalent of Broadway in New York, people would come talk to me about their problems and issues, their families, their love lives, their careers. I found that if I concentrated I could tap into their minds, into their memories, and gain the same information I would get spontaneously at other times, simply by asking for it. I learned that if we are open to hearing messages from the Invisible World, if we are not afraid, we can gain information that will broaden our perception and provide healing.

You may wonder how I could do this—and there's no easy answer. Essentially, the world, and all the people in it, are made up of energy and matter. Whether we can accept it, we are all made up of molecules that are frantically vibrating and we each vibrate at different levels; we are all operating at different frequencies. Our perception changes when our vibration changes to a higher level. Psychics work at a higher level of vibration, and therefore a higher level of perception. In addition to seeing things that others can't see, they can also tune into the individual vibrations of other people, much like a radio transmitter. Energy is also contagious—it is a vibration you can actually feel. If someone in a bad mood walks into a room full of people having a good time, everyone will pick up on it right away. Imagine being able to pick up on energy that is far more subtle and imagine that energy being broadcast into your brain at high volume! I can feel people's psychic and physical pain, their negativity, their bitterness, their hidden anger, their bad luck, their past broken bones and broken hearts, and illness or disease that is lying dormant, waiting to strike. I had to protect myself so that negative energy vibrations from other people wouldn't penetrate me. I was usually accurate, however, in my assessments and predictions about people and it gave them fresh insight and helped them make more conscious decisions. I began to see how my gift could help people.

Despite this, my career as a singer was flourishing and I didn't devote myself to this work full-time. To me it was just something to do in my spare time, before or after a show or while I was traveling. It wasn't until I was twenty-one that I came to know the source of the communication from the other side and began to take my gift more seriously.

My Guardian Angel

One music producer who really believed in me, Aurora, became a good friend and she introduced me to the ideas of the nineteenth-century French spiritualist, Allan Kardec. He was a scientist and scholar and the founder of the spiritism movement. Although he's not well known in the United States, in Europe he is considered the person who started the fascination with communicating with the dead. His teachings started a movement that eventually crossed over to America and has clearly grown with time.

Kardec was the first person to create methods for contacting spirits, which he recorded in *The Spirits' Book*, a book on mediums. He created a phenomenon in Paris in the late 1850s with his séances, where everyone would sit around a table and wait for the spirits to speak to them through the sounds of rapping on the table. Spirits would communicate through this rapping by spelling out words using the number of raps that corresponded with the letters of the alphabet. Kardec wrote that you can call someone on the other side if you use a round table, eliminate fear of any kind, and know that there is nothing wrong with creating this type of communication. Getting messages from the souls who have passed on is an extraordinary experience, but you must have an open mind and strong intuition in order to do it.

I confessed to Aurora that I had been hearing a voice since I was a child and she and I decided to have a séance so we could figure out who the voice belonged to. We sat alone at a round table, lit a candle, and asked the voice to talk to us. I had made a large chart with all of the letters of the alphabet and put a small glass in front of the paper, touching the glass lightly with only one finger. After sitting quietly for a few minutes, I felt a strong presence near me and the energy of this presence moved the glass to different letters of the alphabet spelling out words. The voice was speaking so rapidly that the glass was moving very quickly from letter to letter. Aurora was shocked; it was so clear this was an incredible energy reaching out to us and the words that were being spelled out were undeniably from some other source.

The first word that was spelled out was my mother's maiden name, and then he said, "It's me, I'm here, I'm here to help you." I couldn't believe it—the energy we were feeling; the voice that was speaking to us was that of my maternal grandfather!

The things my grandfather told me that night changed my life. He saw the universe very clearly and went into tremendous detail about things I could have never possibly known in the physical world at that time. He also told me amazing things about the universe—that he could look down at the physical plane and see events with no sense of time, in other words, he could see the past, present, and future as if they were all happening at the same time.

I was so overwhelmed by everything that he was telling me that I could barely think. I wrote it all down but it would take many years for me to absorb and understand completely its meaning. That day, my life changed absolutely and everything he told me about my own life and the world has eventually become reality. Day after day, year after year, the things he told me then have come true. And over time I started to go to him, to ask him what I should do in my own life and to find out what was happening in the world.

During this meeting he told me incredible things about my future. He told me I would move across the ocean to another country to a city full of tall buildings and many people. He described a city full of streets named after numbers, with many yellow cars on the streets, and lights at all times of day and night. He described New York City in perfect detail, the streets, the buildings, and the atmosphere, although I had never even seen a picture of New York. Life in Romania at that time under Ceausescu was extremely difficult. There was very little food, no feeling of personal freedom, and an unpredictable and scary political regime. I wouldn't have even been able to imagine leaving Romania then for a life of freedom, in a city like New York.

He told me I was meant to do parapsychological work, that it was my mission, and he assured me that he would always be my guide. He told me I would meet a lot of influential people, that I would be on television in the new country, that I would make predictions on television and have a tremendous impact on people's lives. He told me I would write a book about all of my experiences and the things that he told me. I was never inclined to write a book so I thought this was very far-fetched. Remember at that time I was a singer, not a writer, nor a well-known psychic.

He told me details about his own life, my family's life—things no one in my family had told me before. He told me he had a castle called Ciucea, the only castle in Transylvania other than the famous Bram Castle that was the castle of Vlad Tepes, who became known in legend as Count Dracula. My grandfather described the interior of the castle to me in exquisite detail: the red fabric on the walls of his bedroom, the letters he had received from other writers he met while living in Paris, the portraits of him as a young man and as an older man, the painting of the woman in the green hat, and the clock with the gold face.

He told me that he had been poisoned by the Communists and he felt the need to be my guardian angel because of the suffering the family had undergone because of him. In my family we didn't talk about him because, even though my mother shared his last name, there was always this fear of danger in being associated with him. My mother had told me her father was the former prime minister of Romania and that he'd been poisoned, but I was told to never say a word.

He also told me he had written and published several books of poetry and even won the National Poetry Prize in 1924, which, at that point, I had known nothing about. His mistake was getting involved in politics. He was meant to be a poet, not a politician, and he got swept up in the political rivalries and ideological differences of the day. He became the prime minister of Romania in 1937 and in 1939 he was was buried.

I asked him why he was telling me all of this, what the purpose was of his communication with me. He explained that if there is something unresolved in a soul's own karma their wish is to stay with us in the other side and protect us. He told me that it was my mission to share the information he gave me with other people to broaden their perceptions and help with their souls' evolution. He also wanted me to help humanity move forward and prevent us from being stuck in darkness and destroying ourselves.

He told me, "The human life on Earth is guided and helped from above. When you leave the Earth your spirit goes through the tunnel of light into different dimensions and perceptions that are infinite worlds all their own. Whatever state of spirit evolution you reach while you're on Earth, whatever level you stop at when you pass over into the Invisible World will affect whether you have to come back. The point of the spirit and of existence is soul evolution. The level of soul evolution you reach, the level of understanding you will gain, depends on the karma you create on the Earth."

He told me that he was watching over me all the time and that he would always be ready to assist me. "I'm at a high level, I can see very well everything that is happening on Earth." I asked him if he would ever come back to Earth in a different body and he replied, "I'll never go back to Earth, but I am at a level where I don't need to go back. It's beautiful and peaceful here and far more interesting than Earth. I'm reading and studying new things and I have no desire to leave it."

Then he said he would always be with me and he was gone. Aurora and I stared at each other in amazement. She had taken down his words and we both looked at them, reading them over and over again, not believing what they said.

After that day, I realized that the guidance of angels watching over us is real and that these angels are karmically connected to us. I hadn't met my grandfather in the physical world, but nonetheless, he had a sense of duty to watch over me and wanted to communicate with me all that he knew so I could share it with others.

My grandfather would continue to guide my life. Years after this séance, I went on tour in New York and I felt very much at home right away and recognized everything my grandfather had described to me years before. I was just coming over for a short time but once I got there, I never left. I've been in New York ever since. My grandfather had described the buildings and atmosphere of New York City with incredible accuracy.

A few years after I had moved to the United States and became well known. I had a friend, a television producer, who went to Ciucea and filmed the interior for a documentary she was working on. The castle had since become a national museum. I watched the film and compared it to my notes from twenty years before and every detail my grandfather had given me was there on film. The letters from his writer friends are under glass in the main hall; the camera spans through the rooms covered with red fabric and focuses on a painting of his wife, all in black except for a bright green hat; there is my grandfather as a young man in a painting hanging on the wall and as an older man in a photograph on the wooden desk. And the camera stops at the tall grandfather clock and rests for a minute on the beautiful gold face.

We All Have Spirit Guides

I've learned so much from my grandfather and after that first direct communication I started to understand the universe and the mysteries of life and death as one unique ongoing process. He helped me to understand who I was and what kind of deeper connection I had with the people in my life. He showed me that we are all much more connected than we realize.

I found that the myth of guardian angels isn't a myth at all; they are real and they are karmically connected to us. Although you may not have met them in the physical world, they have a duty to watch over you that stems from another time. They decide to make it their job. If there is something unresolved in their own karma they make a decision to stay with you and protect you on the other side. It's an amazing feeling to know that someone is there helping you even if during his or her life on earth they were not necessarily responsible or particularly caring toward you. The connection with a soul in the parallel world is also karmic and can help you resolve your karma and evolve.

You may never know who this guide is or was to you but this doesn't matter. On the other side we have no emotions, we have no hatred, we're in peace with everything, so all we can do is love. Guardian angels come and guide the people they have unfinished business with. Sometimes they will decide to communicate with us to help us and therefore resolve their own karma. Sometimes they simply have a message that needs to be delivered. Sometimes they will communicate with us just once, to tell us one piece of needed information. At other times they will give us messages whenever they feel we need them, whenever they think we need to wake up and pay attention to what is happening in our lives.

A spirit is a nonphysical entity that is usually perceived at a higher self level. People who get in touch with them are usually more spiritually and psychically evolved. The more evolved you are, the more you connect at the soul level, at a higher spirit level in the Universe. The purpose of a spirit guide is to help, protect, or assist in someone's spiritual development and to serve as a source of inspiration.

Although getting in touch with those on the other side should come naturally, many times it doesn't because we are skeptical or because we are afraid of what we can't see, so our perception, and therefore the message, is blocked.

I also learned that I can look at other people in the physical world and be aware of whether they have a spirit guide around them. Not everybody does at all times. Often it is up to the spirits to come when they are needed or if called upon in earnest by someone who is seeking guidance. From what I've seen, it appears that from above, from the Invisible World, they can see the future and protect those who are vulnerable, as well as prevent some events. It is wonderful to be protected and loved from beyond, but we must learn to heed the messengers.

I had one client, a woman named Joanne, who came to see me, and I realized right away that there was a spirit around her. I said, "There is a woman here, she says she died young." Joanne stared at me for a minute and then tears came to her eyes. "Yes, my mother died when I was a little girl and I've never known her, never felt her near me."

I nodded. "She talks about Anna alone in another country."

"That's her sister in England."

"She talks about Nicole and Jonathan?"

"That's my sister and her husband." She couldn't believe it.

"She says he is going to move his office."

"Oh my God, Jonathan just told me yesterday that he got a new job and is moving to another office uptown." She seemed convinced. "Carmen, how can I talk to my mother? There are so many things I want to tell her."

"She already knows, Joanne. And you can talk to her anytime you like."

She called me several weeks later to tell me that after so many years of feeling alone and abandoned by her mother that she now felt her mother near her, watching over her with a big smile. She had just taken the bar exam, after failing it once already, and learned that she had passed it. She felt that her mother's presence had helped her pass the exam.

Once a spirit is contacted, even if through someone else such as a psychic or medium, the lines of communication become open and it becomes easier to receive their messages and guidance.

Spirit guides can be helpful as you face different challenges in your life, whether it be raising your kids, accomplishing something important to you, or dealing with grief and loss. They also assist in helping us cross over to the other side at the moment of physical death.

Karmic Family Ties

Although every person has a spirit guide from the moment they are born who is there if needed or called upon, people you know on the physical plane can also pass over and become additional guides. An angel or spirit guide can be the spirit of someone in your family who has passed over to the other side. Somebody who has chosen to stay close to you.

My grandfather was my first spirit guide and now my mother and father are also with me, providing their guidance.

When my father died nine years ago, I got a message from my grandfather, who told me, "When you go home today you'll find your father lying dead on the floor." I went right home and sure enough, my father's body was lying on the floor and there was a big circle of light around him. When I saw it, a chill ran up my spine. He hadn't been sick. He had been feeling well lately; I was not prepared for this. He had died of a heart attack. I was shaken up and was starting to cry when I heard my father's voice tell me, "Don't look at my body, I'm not there anymore. Go to my coat, I tried to write you a note." I checked his coat pocket and there were a few words on paper. He wrote how much he loved me, telling me he would always guide me. He told me not to cry, not to have pain because even though he would no longer be with me physically, his spirit would always be there. After reading the note, I wasn't sad or worried anymore because I knew he was with me. He was telling me it was time for him to go and that it was okay.

Since then I've seen my father many times, often on the other side of the street, and he looks young and content, and although I miss him, I know he's happy where he is. One day, about a month before my mother died, I saw him and he was crying. My mother recently had hip replacement surgery, but other than that she was healthy so at the time I couldn't understand what he was trying to tell me. Afterward, I realized it was his way of warning me so I would be prepared.

Three days before my mother died I sensed it was coming because my house was full of spirits. My mother had had a minor stroke five days earlier and she was in the hospital in a coma. I fervently hoped she would come out of it. When I went home from the hospital everyone in the family who had died was in my house— my aunts and uncles, grandparents, and my father, and I realized they were coming for her, to help her pass over. The day before she died she suddenly woke up out of her coma and said to me, "I'm dead, Carmen." And I told her, "No you're not, Mom."

"Yes, I'm here with my brother and my mother whom I've never met and we're all young and happy. We are all sitting around a table in a beautiful valley with a lot of flowers and a river. But I see my funeral, too. There's a priest with a long beard, and a nun and a child. I don't know who this child is."

I didn't know what she was talking about. I thought she was hallucinating.

"Carmen, everything will be okay. I'm happy here." And she slipped back into a coma. Those were her last words and she died the next day.

After she died I went to St. Mary's church and I spoke to a clean-shaven blond priest and made arrangements for the funeral. Meanwhile my husband had gone, unbeknownst to me, to the other St. Mary's church, the Romanian church, and he had spoken to another priest there and arranged for him to come to the funeral. When I found out, I told my husband to cancel the other priest since I'd already paid the first one so he left him a message not to come. The day of the funeral the blond priest got stuck in traffic and was late, and the other priest, who had never gotten the message, showed up. He had a long beard and he brought with him a nun and a twelve-year-old girl to sing. It was exactly as my mother said it would happen.

My mother continues to guide me in ways that continuously amaze me. In July 2001, *TV Guide* called me to make predictions about which television shows would be successful that coming fall. My mother had been telling me since that spring that Fall 2001 would be full of world problems, and I told *TV Guide* that no one would be watching any new shows in the fall because everyone would be watching the news. I told her there would be major problems in the world and that buildings would be falling down. They thought I was crazy and never ran the interview.

On September 11, I drove my daughter to school at 8:30 A.M. and was driving toward Manhattan for an appointment when my mother's voice came into my mind loud and clear: "Go home and watch the news. Don't go into the city today." I turned the car around, canceled my appointment, and put on the news to see the devastation of the terrorist attacks on the World Trade Center. Sadly, my prediction had come true.

The producer from *TV Guide* later called me in shock, saying she couldn't believe it. And I am grateful to my mother for watching over me.

Communicating with Your Spirit Guide

There are several ways to communicate with your spirit guide, as long as your psychic center is open.

Communication with them is something that can be learned and can be done in different ways. If a spirit wants to communicate, it will usually find a way. Some spirits will feel very strongly that they want to deliver a message and can be very persistent. They can make noise around you, by having an object or a book that has some meaning for you inexplicably fall off of a shelf; they can alter your electric appliances by turning a radio on when a certain song is playing, or a light may start blinking or turn on and off. Sometimes they will come in the form of a scent that appears in the air seemingly out of nowhere—a perfume, a certain food, a cigar or pipe. They may also come to you in a recurring thought or in a dream. Sometimes they are trying to warn you, to tell you to wake up and pay attention to your surroundings or the choices you are making. They are trying to pull you out of the physical into a more spiritual and clearheaded place.

So how can you begin to hear and translate the messages from your spirit guide? How do we know when invisible forces are guiding us? My entire life I knew that there was somebody there because I was constantly being sent the right messages at the right time about what was going to happen next.

Often a message from the other side will come in the form of a blessing or an obstacle. If we are on the right path and doing what we are supposed to be doing, life will go easier. If we are heading down the wrong road, life will be more difficult. If things in any given situation are going smoothly, if things fall naturally into place, it is meant to be and you are on the right path. If you are caught in a situation of emotional turmoil, or if your ego has taken over, or if you find that something you are trying to accomplish is more difficult than it should be, that too many obstacles have come across your path, stop and ask yourself why. Your spirit knows, your intuition knows, but you have to be awake enough, and have enough self-awareness, to hear the message.

For example, you may be in a relationship where there is always conflict, where the two of you never can agree or are constantly fighting. This type of constant fighting is an obstacle. I have a client, Carol, who lived with a man for six years, and although they felt that they loved each other, they were constantly fighting. Despite this, they stayed together, but they never made the commitment to actually get married because each time they felt closer to one another and things were going smoothly, there would be another fight that would set them back. I told Carol many times that this type of constant stress and arguing wasn't good for her and that if the relationship was meant to be she wouldn't have spent six years fighting with the man. If two people truly love each other, they care about each other enough to find proper ways to resolve disagreements. A relationship should be a support system, not a constant source of stress. Carol finally found the courage to leave her boyfriend and within six months met another man that she became engaged to shortly after meeting. If there are too many obstacles in your path, take a step back and look at the larger picture. You may be getting a message that something isn't meant to be. When things are meant to be, they aren't so difficult, they flow easier. This can happen in regards to finding a place to live, what you choose to study in school, finding a job or career, and choosing the person you marry. Things that are meant to be move with ease and grace, and those that aren't are filled with obstacles.

Understanding the messages from beyond depends on the depth of our own perception and spiritual evolution. We get messages every minute of our lives, even during insignificant events. So how do we establish communication between ourselves and our messengers? How do we make a connection? We tend to "shoot the messenger," usually by ignoring them, but not only shouldn't you "shoot" them, you should listen to them, be nice to them, honor them, and take heed! What they say can change your life.

Too often we don't see the synchronicity in our own

lives or read the signs as we pass them on the road of life. We walk around oblivious, asleep, and then live our lives in a confused state wondering, "Why is this happening to me?" Why are some people more in tune with their messengers and others not? It isn't just a gift, it's a matter of paying attention, of being awake, of not being afraid of what we might hear. Some people call it intuition or gut instinct and it is that, but it's also much more.

Ask for Guidance, then Read the Signs

Often it is just a case of asking for guidance and then waiting for signs to appear. Sometimes when we focus too hard on a problem or try to figure it out we'll never find the answer. Ask your spirit a specific question and then leave it alone and wait for a message.

Have you ever awakened in the middle of the night with a "Eureka"—a seemingly sudden answer to a problem you're having? Or you're walking down the street running errands, and the answer will simply come into your mind. That's a message. Often when you empty your mind, and your emotions and ego are calm, you are more open to hearing what you need to hear.

We've all heard the phrase, "There's no such thing as a coincidence" but what does it really mean? What you may think is a coincidence is really a message. Pay attention and ask yourself, "What is the message; what is this coincidence trying to tell me?" The same goes for spontaneous thoughts that seem to come "out of the blue." Sometimes a certain thought will pop into your head and shed light on a situation or it will be a small voice telling you what you're about to do isn't right.

Dreams

Another powerful way to receive messages is through dreams. Often we forget our dreams when we wake up and later in the day the memory of our dream will come into our conscious mind. Pay attention to that—it means the message came to you twice, once in your subconscious dream and again in your conscious waking world. Other times the message in a dream will be so powerful it will wake us from a deep sleep. Write it down and pay attention. Dreams often share messages in symbols or symbolic figures and situations. Keep a notebook by your bed and write your dreams down and go back later and try to interpret their messages. Dreams can express anxieties and fears, or share with you your deepest hopes, or knowledge you won't accept while awake. Sometimes a spirit guide will actually appear in your dream and tell you something directly. This is perhaps the most powerful kind of dream message.

Déjà Vu

Déjà vu is also a potent message. You find yourself in a situation that seems familiar or you meet a person and you feel that you know them. You know you haven't met them in this life, not in the physical world, but experiencing déjà vu is often a memory from a past life or a spirit guide trying to make you notice something or somebody. It's a connection to the past, to the memory, and to the other side.

For example, when I was a young girl just beginning to sing on the stage, I used to close my eyes while I was performing and I always had this image of a tall woman with a big hat singing opera. I didn't know who this woman was but for some reason her image always came to me and she was always dressed in eighteenth-century theatrical costume.

The first time I went to Paris I passed a theater and felt I had been there before, even though I knew I hadn't been in this life. When I passed this theater years later, the image of this woman came back to me. I went into the theater and found out it had been an opera house in the last century. Then I passed an old townhouse and recognized it, feeling I had been in that house before. I strongly believe that my musical career was something I carried over from a past life. I think there were enough signs on this trip that were sending me a message. I believe I was the tall woman in the costume; was a French opera singer in a past life. Later on that same trip, Stella Simonetti, an opera singer who was performing in France at that time, heard me sing, and told me I had two voices; the voice I used in my popular albums and that of an incredible soprano. Although I didn't use my soprano voice, the talent was there and I believe that gift had carried over from my past life into this one.

Synchronicities

There is a certain perfection in the universe that becomes clear to us when we pay attention to synchronicity. Synchronicity is when things or events happen at the same time, or in such a way that you can see that they are parallel. This synchronicity—what we usually call being "in sync"—is a message that events are unfolding according to the rules of the Universe.

For example, after my mother's death, I went through all of her papers and found my parents' birth certificates and their marriage certificate. My father died when he was seventy years old—actually he was seventy years and seven months. My mother also died at seventy years and seven months. They were seven years and seven months apart in age. She died on November 8, which would have been the fiftieth anniversary of her marriage to my father. So her death and marriage were on the same date. I married my husband on November 8 and both of my daughters, Alexandra and Carmen, were born on November 8. That is synchronicity at work.

Mediums

One of the most obvious and popular ways to receive messages is to go to a medium. Most mediums are thought to be healers because they open the lines of communication and can help the grieving process by resolving feelings of guilt, remorse, or confusion after someone has passed on. Having one final good-bye or saying the things that you weren't able to say to the loved one when they were living is a spiritual healing. The more evolved the medium, the more information you will receive.

Mediums work by creating a connection with the spiritual world and usually it is up to the spirit, not the medium, as to whether they want to communicate. Sometimes the spirit that comes through is not who you thought you wanted to talk to, but they are there to share a message nonetheless. The medium goes into a state of self-hypnosis and regulated breathing that creates an altered state of consciousness through which the spirit speaks. Typically, mediums always remember what was said through them.

Mediums work in different ways. They may use one or any combination of the following techniques:

MENTAL VISION—This is when an image comes into the medium's mind and they describe it. This is how I usually work; I work with visions; I see things. Typically mental visions come in the form of symbols, a letter representing someone's name, or a meaningful object or event. An image will come into my mind and then I will describe it to my client. For me this image means nothing, but it always has some significance to the person who is trying to connect to the spirit.

AUTOMATISMS—This is when a message comes through automatic writing. When I say this, I mean that the medium is putting pen to paper but the words that are written come from the spirit. George Anderson uses this technique; he takes a pen and paper and the spirit communicates through him in words on paper. This is also how I communicated with my grandfather that first time.

PSYCHOMETRY—This is when a medium communicates with a soul that has passed over by holding an object that once belonged to them when they were in a physical body, such as a piece of jewelry, clothing, or even a photograph. After entering a meditative state, the medium will hold this object and begin to receive messages in the form of thoughts or emotions.

CLAIRAUDIENCE—This is when there is a combination of a mental vision and hearing things but the focus is on the messages the medium hears. For example, John Edward hears things. A spirit talks directly to the medium with a specific message they want to get across.

CLAIRVOYANCE—This is similar to having a mental vision but it is more complex, when the medium can see, hear, and project a specific spirit. For example, I've had clients come in and a spirit will appear, even though the client has come to me for a different reason. They will appear much as they did on the physical plane and they are usually standing near a door or sitting on a chair. They will have a very clear message to get across and will talk to the other person through me.

Meditation

You can also find your own spirit guides and communicate with them through regular and specific meditations. Your success will really depend on how open you are and how much you believe. If your psychic center is open you can also get in touch faster. Sometimes it can take a few minutes, sometimes several days, as some days you are more open than others.

Try the following meditation as a way to open your psychic center and connect.

To get in touch with a spirit guide you have to go beyond the limitations of the physical mind and create a mental state that is open to the Invisible World. The best way is to go into a state of deep relaxation and sharpened awareness.

First, find a place that is quiet, away from other people and distractions. Take a photograph of the person you'd like to communicate with and put it in front of you, on the ground or on a table, and light a candle next to it. Make sure the candle is far enough away so the flame doesn't ignite the photograph! If you have an object of theirs, a piece of jewelry, clothing, or any type of object,

---

sit and look at the photograph and the flame, and hold the object in your hand. Sit quietly for a few minutes and relax, regulate your breathing, and go back into your memory to the person's presence while they were here. Eliminate any feelings of fear; there is no reason to fear.

Talk to the spirit. Tell him or her that you love him or her and let him or her know that you are open to hearing what he or she has to say. Then ask for guidance. You can address specific problems or just ask him or her to listen. You will sense a powerful energy around you. Sometimes the spirit you call will come and sometimes he or she won't. Sometimes you'll ask for someone specific and a different spirit will show up. Relax and attend to the voices or images that come into your consciousness. Certain words, images, or feelings may come to you. Pay attention to those images, words, or feelings. What comes to you from beyond this world is often the truth. It can be the truth we are afraid to face in this world.

Write down the words, images, and feelings you receive. Thank the spirit, tell him or her you love and appreciate his or her guidance. Then blow out the candle.

The more you practice the more you will receive and the easier it will be to record the messages. Although the significance of the message may not be immediately apparent, keep a journal with these messages written down and refer to them. You will be amazed by what you learn.

*U*ltimately the point of communicating with a spirit guide or retrieving messages sent from the Invisible

World is to achieve awareness. They may help you gain self-awareness or a broader perception; they may serve to comfort you or to help you prepare for curves coming up on life's road. They may also just be wake-up calls to make you pay attention to what's going on in your life, to stop and reassess your direction, to snap you out of your comfort zone, to pay attention to the people around you. The awareness these messages create is meant to help you understand your own karma. And it is only in understanding your karma that you can propel your spiritual evolution by beginning the work it takes to resolve it. But what exactly is karma?

CHAPTER THREE

Resolving Your Karma

When someone comes to see me, I can tell as soon as they walk in the door if they have heavy karma. I can tell just by looking at them. They have the weight of the world on their shoulders, they are down, they have a scowl on their faces. They are unhappy, they are afraid, they complain about all of their problems. You may think, "Yes, Carmen, we can all tell if someone is unhappy," but I am talking about an unhappiness that goes deeper than appearances. Many of my clients are extremely successful. They are wealthy; they're in good health; they are beautiful; they are famous; and the outside world may not recognize their bad karma. These external benchmarks of happiness do not mean that someone is happy at the level of their soul.

Then there are the clients who come in who feel they have more problems than everyone else, and a lot of the time they're right. I hear phrases from them like, "I'm unlucky." "Life threw me a curve ball." "What did I do to deserve this?" "Nothing ever works out for me." or "It isn't my fate to be happy." These people feel victimized; they are confused and don't understand why things never seem to go their way. They, too, have bad karma.

Karma is a complex thing—we all have it—we are born with certain karma and we also create our own karma—and some of us have more bad than good. What I try to help people understand is that no matter how bad their karma may be, there is a way to resolve it, there is a way to change their "luck" and turn their lives around to go the way they want them to.

What Is Karma?

Although karma has become a popular concept in the West, it is actually one of the world's oldest concepts from one of the world's oldest cultures, Hinduism. In Sanskrit karma means "deeds" or "actions"; it comes from the root "kri" which means "to do." It is the mental and physical deeds that determine the effects of your life and rebirth and can be consequences from your previous lives or from actions in this one.

In Eastern cultures, and more recently in Western

culture, there is a strong belief that the soul travels from one body to the next. The force that drives the process of rebirth of the soul is an element of karma. Karma is when the actions of the previous life are carried over in the present one, or when the actions of this life are carried over into the next. Reincarnation comes from the Latin word, *căro* which means to be in the flesh, and "re" which means again. So reincarnation is simply "to be in the flesh again." It reinforces what I've said about the soul never dying and the fact that the soul is far more important than the physical body. The body is temporal; the soul is infinite. Human beings come into a body alone and when we shed our body we die alone. The only thing we take with us are our memories, our karma.

I like to think of karma as memory. Every thought and action, everything you do, creates memory, like data in a computer. This data or memory is either positive or negative. All of the negative memory will resurface in your life, again and again, and the only way to move forward is to resolve it. Your life is a process of resolving karmic issues and in doing so you grow and move on. Unresolved karma breeds negative energy, disease, and unhappiness. Many of the things that go wrong in your life are a result of unresolved karma.

In America karma is best expressed in popular phrases like, "what goes around, comes around" and "what you sow, you will reap." Karma has also been referred to as having a "boomerang effect" where the thoughts and actions that you send out into the world turn around and come back at you. In the New Testament, Jesus says, "Do unto others as you would have them do unto you." Karma goes a step further and dictates that "What you do unto others will come back to you." I think Jesus and the Hindus really had the same idea. Think about that the next time you want to say or do something nasty to someone else!

If you understand that the whole world is a circle of energy that never ends—with energy, memory, and information moving constantly within it—you can see how all that same information, positive or negative, is energy moving around in the sphere that is your life. The things you think and do will come back to either bless you or haunt you. We are each responsible for our own thoughts and actions and karma explains that in many cases our own pain and suffering is a result of our wrongdoing. This is what makes us unique and composes our lives. It also creates a field of information around us at the level of energy. We store this information in our field; it is like data in a computer.

We have many different ways of action—through our thoughts, our speech, and what we do with our hands. It is a negative or positive thought, a kind or unkind word, a caring caress or a hurtful punch. If you free yourself from hate, desire, disillusionment, and all negative emotions, you have freed yourself from the law of cause and effect. If you continue to hate, and desire what you don't have, and think in negative thought patterns, you will remain trapped.

Many times, I think in the West particularly, people confuse karma with fate or destiny. Karma is not fate or destiny; it is cumulative memory. And karma is not something "fixed"—you have control over it to some extent. Or at least you have the control to change it by changing your thoughts and actions and also by creating awareness of past karma and working to resolve it.

Fate is, as I like to put it, the "data in your computer." What I mean is that there is a certain degree of preordained "facts" about your life. These are the day that you're born, your place of birth, the timing of the death of your parents, the timing of your own death, and certain elements of your health. These are all unchangeable facts and we have to go through these certain events as lessons. It is the foundation on which we grow. Fate is the events we will experience in our lives that cannot be changed—we simply must go through them and learn from them. Because of our own lack of perception we often think of ourselves as victims of fate.

But we aren't victims of fate because there is another factor at play in our lives—*destiny*. Destiny is the things that we can change of our own free will. For example, we can choose to marry, to have children, to use our skills and talents, to resolve our own karma. The more we take control of our individual destiny, the easier it is for us to deal with our fate.

Karma is the combination of thoughts and actions that help us deal with our fate and create our destiny. It was my fate to be born in Romania but it was my destiny to become a singer, travel around the world, and move to America. I had no control over where I was born, but I did have control over where I would eventually end up. It was my thoughts and actions—my karma—that created my destiny.

The Three Levels of Karma

In the Sanskrit dictionary there are twenty-five definitions of different types of karma. Karma is such a central concept in Hindu culture that it is like the Eskimos having so many different words for snow! For our purposes I'm going to explain just three different types of karma.

Present Karma (Agami)

Agami takes place in the present and is everything you do today that creates cause and effect in the future. Whether you realize it or not, every day you are creating karma with every thought and action. If you kill a flower or a bug, yell at your spouse, hate yourself when you look in the mirror and call yourself fat or ugly, are jealous of a friend, shove somebody on the subway, behave dishonestly (even if it's just keeping the extra change from the store clerk), you are creating bad karma. All of this negative thinking and action creates negative memory in your subconscious. It is stored in your brain. Every day there are a million activities in the brain that can create bad karma.

On the other hand, every single thing you do each day that is positive—aiding a beggar, helping a friend by making a phone call for them, running an errand or bringing food to someone who is sick, saying a kind word to a stranger, showing love and affection—creates good karma. Life is a constant balancing act of offsetting the bad karma with the good. With every thought, word, and action you are making a choice of which kind of karma you create in your life.

For example, when Joan came to see me she was working at a nightclub as a waitress. The club needed another woman to work there as a hostess, but because of her own insecurity, she said she would do both jobs to avoid any possible competition. She started working crazy hours, seven days a week, and after a few months she got sick from working so much. Her boss had to hire someone while she was out and he hired Patty, a much younger woman, to be the hostess.

When Joan went back to work she went in with the attitude that Patty was the enemy. She hated Patty, treated her badly, deliberately made things difficult for her. Every day Joan would call me and ask, "When is Patty going to leave the club?" She thought if Patty would just quit, she could have peace of mind. I told her, "You will only have peace of mind if you stop seeing this woman as a threat and start treating her like a friend. Only in making peace with her will you evolve." She didn't listen to me. She started to fight with her boss and she treated Patty so badly that ultimately, she was fired. She would call me and try to blame Patty for getting her fired. I told her, "This event will repeat itself in your life over and over again until you stop your jealous and hateful behavior. You've ruined your career and you've turned your life into a hell." She was finally able to see that she had created this situation herself; it was her own thoughts and actions that led to her being miserable and getting fired. She created her karma in the present and the only way she could resolve it was by acknowledging her role in creating it, apologizing to Patty, and entering her next job with a different frame of mind.

When we start the day, every day, we need to be aware of how important our thoughts and behavior are. The way we look at our life and those around us is constantly creating karma.

Past Karma (Prarabdha)

This is karma from the past, karma that has already been created, things that you've already done. The things you feel today are the effects of your past actions. This karma has already been set in motion and is the consequence that you are left to deal with. This type of karma is also a part of our day every day. If your past thoughts and actions were positive, then you reap the rewards and if they were negative, you are paying the consequences. This is the combination of all the karma of this life and past lives that has been set loose into the present.

In Bistrita, the small town where I grew up, there was a bakery near the train station that was owned by a middle-aged woman. One day a seven-year-old boy came in hungry and took a bagel and tried to run away. The woman was angry and ran after him. Instead of speaking gently to the boy and asking him why he was stealing and teaching him a lesson, she started to wring his neck and screamed at him that the police would kill him for stealing. The boy was terrified and when he escaped from her hands he was so blind with fear that he ran right onto the train tracks and was killed by an oncoming train.

The boy's mother was devastated, of course, and she went to the bakery crying and told the woman, "You killed my son and because of your cruelty you will lose what you love the most."

Years went by and nothing happened. The woman at the bakery had a little niece who was sweet and pretty and loved her aunt, and the woman loved this little girl more than anything in the world. The little girl would sit in the bakery all day and keep her aunt company. When the girl was seven she was hit by a bus right in front of the bakery. The woman ran outside and the little girl died in her arms. This was a terrible tragedy and when it happened the entire town remembered the boy who had died years before and the words of his mother.

Accumulated Karma (Sanchita)

Sanchita is karma that accumulates over time, and sometimes over many lifetimes. You could say it works like the "snowball effect." In every day of our lives, in everything that we do, karma is created. If we don't erase it or heal it at the end of every day, it will accumulate and become bigger. Negative action will multiply from the moment it is committed. Think about telling a lie. If you tell one small lie you will most likely have to create more lies to protect yourself from being found out. Over time all of these lies can accumulate into one big lie and you are no longer living a life of integrity. This lie will be with you at all times and the consequences of not telling the truth will only get worse.

You need to pray at night or purify every night to heal all that you've done over the course of that day. Otherwise your negative karma grows, and the more it grows the more difficult it is to heal. Left unresolved, it may never be healed, and you will have to live with the consequential suffering. The longer you refuse to acknowledge karma, the harder it becomes to recognize and identify, and ultimately, the more difficult it becomes to resolve.

The Importance of Resolving Karma

In order to move forward you have to heal karma and this can only be accomplished if you acknowledge that the quality and the condition of your life is determined by your own actions. This is very important; if you acknowledge that your peace of mind is a result of everything you've ever done before, then you have the key to your own life and even your previous lives. The purpose of doing this isn't to blame yourself and sink into a hole of self-blaming despair. The point is to be honest with yourself, to view your life objectively, and use your new awareness to move forward by healing the past and making the right changes for the future. The way to do this is to act in accordance with the Universal Laws.

I will discuss the Universal Laws in more detail in the next chapter, but understand that in order to survive and be in harmony with the universe we need to act in accordance with the laws. If the universe is divine, full of harmony and perfection and love and beauty—which I believe it is—then we are each a particle of the divine and indirectly considered to be divine. Each and every one of us is part of the greater whole and it is important that we maintain a unity with the whole, that we keep our individual fields of information in synch, in balance with the Universal Laws. If you resist or try to operate against the Universal Laws, you end up in conflict.

Releasing ourselves from bad karma is the only way to reach eternity, to achieve immortality. When you acknowledge the divine in yourself and tap into it you become immortal. Most of us fail to realize this. The divine, the soul is timeless.

The way to heal karma is through forgiveness of

yourself and your own actions, and learning the lessons you need to learn. You also heal karma by forgiving the actions of the other people in your life. In doing so you create peace within yourself and in the world, and ultimately, you gain wisdom.

All theories about karma agree that playing out your karma, healing your karma, can span many lives. Reincarnation is one opportunity to repair what you did wrong. It is an opportunity to come back and repent, to ask for forgiveness and change what you did wrong, especially on actions that purposely held ill intention. The attainment of enlightenment removes the accumulated bad karma of the past and eliminates the need to reincarnate, to come back. If you look at some people who are old and unhappy with the way their life has been, they will need to come back because they are leaving this world with many things unresolved. They haven't learned the lessons they came here to learn. The opportunity to come back is given to those souls who didn't know how to handle their own lives. However, you don't need to wait for another lifetime to resolve past karma—the purpose of this book is to show you how to resolve your karma now!

Ultimately, life is a process of learning and every night before we go to sleep we need to go into an introspection of our daily thoughts and actions, every day of our life we have to make peace with the things we did that day and with the people we interacted with. We have to take time out to summarize our thoughts and actions. If you pray and heal your karma every day you will be happier. Based on this knowledge, I created my Karmic Resolution Method, which is included in the last chapter of this book. Joan used this Method to acknowledge and resolve the karma she had created with Patty.

This Method is all about being honest with yourself and trying to always look into the self for answers to life's problems. If you look within the self, you will find the answer because all the answers lie within—it's just a matter of learning how to recognize the answers. Listening to your messengers, your spirit guides, is one way to find the answers. But you can't just sit back and wait for a spirit guide to tell you what to do—you need to learn how to listen to that voice that is within.

It is my understanding that karmic things need to be resolved, they have beginnings and ends, they aren't forever. So the very moment karmic issue is resolved in your life, you can move to another level, another karma or event. Metaphorically, resolving our karma is like attending school and karmic events are the lessons of life. As I saw on the other side, although our spiritual lives survive in the universe for all eternity, our physical existence's sole purpose is for learning and soul evolution. The field of information that stores everything about us, all of our needs and our emotions, our past experiences, everything that has ever been absorbed by us, affects how we behave day to day; it affects our decisions and actions and reactions to life's events. If we find that we repeatedly make bad choices or decisions or react poorly or negatively to what is happening in our lives the only way to create change is to go into that field of information and analyze it.

The Three Types of Karma

Individual

Individual karma is the karma of any given person; it is your unique karma, the karma you have created or must resolve in your lifetime.

There are a lot of people in this life who are negative, jealous, skeptical, and they live in a circle of darkness that affects them, their families, and their friends. I read into their memories, I introspect, I investigate, to find what these people are all about, and then I come to know the roots to their problems, the context in which they live and their level of perception. I can read this all in their field of information. We all are capable of doing this but most of us have so much information around us that we don't acknowledge or pay attention to it.

Unfortunately for most people, it is impossible for them to recognize their own karma. When people come to me for predictions I cannot begin to tell them about their future until I know where they are right now, and where they have been. I must look at the present karma, the past karma, and the accumulated karma and then I can begin to see what the future holds. The past karma is going to affect the future.

One of the reasons so many of my clients have major breakthroughs is because I acknowledge their negative karma and am not afraid to tell them that they are stuck in it.

Reading the future can be tricky. I never go there until I've figured out where you are right now, at this point in your evolution and level of self-understanding. First, we must travel very far back to look at everything you have gone through in this lifetime and even before. Some of you have been trapped for a long, long time, but I believe it is always possible to find lost memory, resolve karma, and move forward. If you are looking for easy predictions, projections and visions of the future, I can't help you. However, if you are willing to dig deeply into your soul and explore your true self, you can learn how to resolve painful karmic issues.

Our tendency is to blame others for our problems, but the truth is that we often create our own karma. Our problem is that we don't want to see that; we don't want to look at ourselves and take responsibility for our own thoughts, actions, and hence, our karma.

Most of us blame the world around us, the world on the outside, for our problems, instead of the world on the inside. The world outside is often just a reflection of what's going on in our inner world. So resolving karma—what may look to you like outside forces working against you—is really a matter of digging deep inside, to the level of your soul. That's why it's important that the individual alone is responsible for his or her own karma.

Now, I'm not trying to place blame on people for events that are clearly out of their control; I'm not trying to say that if something bad happens to you, it's your own fault. There are things in our lives that we can control and there are even more that we can't. There is plenty of random violence, evil, illness, and loss in the world and we can take action to avoid these things or protect against them, but none of us are immune. We will all face suffering in our lives. When I talk about karma, I am talking about your *own* actions and your *own* thoughts and responses and how they affect *your* future.

A case in point is Elena, a woman who came to see me for a first reading and before she even crossed the room I could feel her bad karma, the negative energy surrounding her. She was attractive, in her late fifties, I guessed, extremely well dressed and well groomed and she clearly had money, but something about her was very off.

She sat down and fidgeted with her designer handbag for a minute before blurting out, "I came to see if you could tell me how long my husband is going to live."

Rather than directly answering her question I smiled and said, "Why don't you let me do a reading on you first and then we can discuss your husband." A reading is essentially gathering information and then analyzing it to reveal the cycle of your life and to assess where you are now.

She agreed, so I asked for her birthdate, held her left hand in both of mine, closed my eyes, and went into a quiet meditative state, feeling her energy. Almost immediately I was barraged with images.

"You and your husband are not happy. You've been married for over thirty years but it isn't a good marriage . . . He has cheated on you. He is a successful man, a rich man, but he has been abusive to you . . . by this I mean emotionally and physically abusive." She nodded in amazement.

Once I get started I tend to talk very quickly, sometimes moving rapidly from subject to subject in accordance with all the images I'm seeing. "You are having problems with your health. Problems with your scalp, your hair has been falling out, and with your teeth. You are having stomach problems and sleeping problems." Again, she nodded. "You have a child, a daughter. She is very difficult for you to handle. The two of you are not getting along."

She nodded, clearly upset with having her problems discussed out loud.

"But I see that you are in the mental health field, and have been for some time. You are a therapist?"

She hesitated and looked at me, as if contemplating whether she had told this to me in our initial phone call to schedule a meeting. "Yes, I've been a therapist for twenty-five years. I have a very successful practice."

"You spend your professional life trying to help others solve their problems and yet you feel stuck yourself. You are feeling trapped in your own life."

She burst into tears. "Yes! I hate my husband. I've hated him almost since we got married. We barely speak to each other. He's been sleeping with our cleaning lady and doesn't even try to hide it. If only he would die I know I could be happy. Why is this happening to me?"

"If you've been this unhappy with him for so many years and haven't been able to resolve your problems, why don't you just leave him?"

"I can't," she cried. "All of our property and money are in his name."

Can you imagine waking up every day for thirty-five years hating the person you live with? Here was a woman with a twelve-room house on Park Avenue, who had a successful therapy practice, could afford the most beautiful clothes and haircuts, the most relaxing spa treatments, and had all the comfort and luxury that money could buy, but she woke up every morning with hate in her heart. All she could think of was that if her husband would just die she would finally be happy. What Elena didn't understand was that her unhappiness was caused by her own unresolved karma—karma that had accumulated and festered over many years.

Elena created her own karma thirty-five years before by refusing to acknowledge that she married for the wrong reasons. That one action created a toxic chain of events that led her to my door.

Elena came to me to predict her future, but as long as she only looked at the effect—"I hate my husband"—rather than the cause, she could never crawl out of her self-inflicted hell. Her bad karma would contaminate everything—her health would get worse, her relationship with her husband and daughter would get worse—and it would become harder and harder for her to turn her life around.

I didn't predict her husband's death because I knew Elena was asking the wrong question. This prediction could never help her move toward karmic healing and closer to finding her own way. Instead, I brought her back to her everyday life, her problems, her responsibilities. I gently pushed her to connect with her own memories and her truth. I could see what she refused to see for herself. Instead of asking, "When will my husband die?" she should have asked, "How can I go on living with this murderous rage in my heart?" I knew that if she continued on this negative path, her own mind would destroy her.

Could someone like Elena, with so much accumulated rage and bad karma, find her way to resolution? Perhaps, but not until she recognized that every hateful thought she had toward her husband boomeranged back to her.

It took Elena a long time to get "unstuck." Over several sessions I was able to "read" her and give her my insights, but ultimately, she had to do her own work. I gave her several meditation exercises and walked her through my Karmic Resolution Method, and eventually she began to change. One day she looked at me with a dazed expression and said, "Carmen, what took me so long? I'm leaving it all behind me." She was finally ready to walk away from the marriage, the millions, the poisonous rage, and the trap of bad karma. With compassion and understanding she was able to forgive herself and everyone else—her husband, her daughter, even the cleaning lady. She had broken the pattern by seeing that the problem was in her, in her emotions, and in her attachment to her lifestyle. "I can't wait to move on and live my life—I feel free as a bird," she told me in a breathless voice.

Family Karma

Family Karma is karma that is created within the family dynamic, within the cycle of the family. I've always believed that we are everything our ancestors have ever done; we are a result of all this, which is why our lives and our every action will reflect later in our children and grandchildren. Karma can be passed down to or transferred to you from your parents or grandparents and, in turn, you can pass it down to your children. Haven't you ever had the feeling that things were just escalating negatively in your life and you didn't know where it was all coming from? It may be family karma. Many of the famous families we know have family karma.

For example, the Kennedy family has often been called "cursed" because of the unusually high number of premature deaths, tragedies, and scandals that have all taken place within this high profile family. JFK and Robert Kennedy were both assassinated; Ted Kennedy has been haunted his entire life by the incident at Chappaquiddick; William Kennedy Smith was tried for rape; and of course, there was the tragic death of JFK Jr. in a plane crash. Sadly, I predicted JFK Jr.'s death on a couple of occasions. In 1997, the day after Princess Diana died in a tragic car accident, I went on television on ABC's "Let's Talk" and said that Mother Teresa would die within a week, and she did. I then said that the next internationally famous person who would die unexpectedly and draw a lot of attention and public sympathy was a young man who would die in an airplane crash in two years. That was JFK Jr. Actually, the year before, in 1996, I repeatedly told Carolyn Bessette Kennedy's sister, Lauren, not to fly in a plane. She said, "Carmen, that's ridiculous, I have to fly all the time. I don't believe you." She stopped coming to see me shortly after that. Three years later she died with JFK Jr. and her sister in the crash. I was filled with terrible sadness when I heard this.

The Kennedy family isn't so much "cursed" as they are dealing with accumulated family karma that has been passed down for generations. There is karma in the past because of someone's past actions and everyone becomes affected. A very few family members can escape, like Caroline Kennedy who has lived through tremendous tragedy and has managed to keep her own life positive.

For some families, it is one tragedy after another—early tragic deaths, alcoholism, scandals—nothing works for them. What's going on in that family? Where is it coming from? It stays for generations and perpetuates itself, until there's awareness, acknowledgment for the need for forgiveness, and until the collective consciousness of the family tries to resolve the karma together. Otherwise it will stay there and multiply.

One of my dearest clients and friends is a beautiful woman with a beautiful soul. I'll call her Georgia. She comes from a wealthy, accomplished family and her ancestors were one of the first founding families in America. She has grown up with extreme privilege and unlimited amounts of money. She went to the best schools, she had a choice of careers, and she lives in a beautiful house. And yet, Georgia does not feel that her life is blessed. She has everything in the material world, but she doesn't feel loved. Her parents were unfaithful to one another and divorced and remarried other people more than once. All of her family members are unkind to one another; they're all jealous, and all they care about is their money. Consequently there have been many tragic deaths, fights, and breakups and general unhappiness through many generations. No one in this family is happy, no one feels loved, and Georgia has never had a satisfying relationship. She feels that no man loves her just for herself: every relationship ends badly and she feels she will never be happily married.

Georgia hasn't brought any of this on herself and she spent many years struggling as a confused and lost soul wondering why nothing developed for her. I have been working with her for the past several years and she has evolved spiritually and become more at peace as she has come to understand the extent of her accumulated family karma. She and I learned that two hundred years ago, her great grandfather killed a man, and the wife and son of this murdered man cursed him and all of his children. For the next two hundred years the family has suffered. It wasn't the curse from this woman that ruined his life and that of his descendants, it was the karma that his action—the actual murder—created. Once Georgia came to see her problems in this context, she was able to develop more objectivity and more awareness, and to focus not on the suffering but on the things she could do in her own life to break the bad karma. Resolving family karma is in some ways more difficult than resolving your individual karma, because family karma can be more difficult to recognize.

Group Karma

Karma also explains a lot of the problem imbalances, inequalities and injustices of mankind. Entire groups of people and the places they live can have their own karma. The planet Earth has memory, and different places on Earth have memory, even our Milky Way has memory. And like all karma, the longer that a group of people or a place live with bad karma without resolving it, the more it will accumulate. Group karma can stay in an area for thousands of years.

For example, the Middle East has been experiencing bad karma for thousands of years and with every passing year that this karma is not resolved, it accumulates and grows worse. We've all seen this as the Middle East sinks further and further into chaos. At some level it makes sense that this is happening because the Middle East is essentially where the disconnect between man and the divine first took place thousands of years ago. All of the wars and religions that divided people stem from the Middle East and when you look at the wars that continue there today they are mostly wars about religious differences. Instead of allowing the divine within us to pull all of us together, we allow it to break us apart. In the name of God we kill one another ruthlessly and foolishly, and so the karma continues and the differences become stronger and harder to resolve.

To understand the Invisible World and the divine we have to understand that God is not an old man with a white beard who sits lording over all of humanity. Rather, God, or what so many of us have gotten used to calling God, is actually the divine principle of all our being. Our life here is to learn how to reach God, how to reach the divine principle through our thoughts, deeds, and actions, but instead we do the opposite; we use God as an excuse to kill and destroy one another. This type of ignorance will be our own undoing unless we wake up, acknowledge our bad karma and begin to resolve it.

When I talk about prediction for prevention, nowhere does this come more into effect than in group karma. I've been asked many times on television, "What will happen in the Middle East?" which to me is an easy question—it's going to get worse. It's going to escalate. And so it has. How can it not with several thousand years of unresolved karma there? Resolving such long-lasting negative group karma is a very long and arduous process, especially if there is no awareness of it. Yugoslavia has suffered bad karma since the First World War, in conflicts that continue to this day. We are all still reeling from the karma we created during the Second World War with the Holocaust and persecution of the Jews and the dropping of the atomic bomb. Each action creates ripple effects of consequences and our world becomes a more and more complicated and difficult place in which to live. The only way to resolve group karma is through our evolution as a species, through our spiritual development and through spiritual awareness at the level of the collective consciousness.

The Five Keys to Healing

The way we heal our bad karma is also the way we learn about ourselves, evolve spiritually and move into the rest of our lives. They are one and the same. In my Karmic Resolution Method I provide a daily process that helps you do this. At the foundation of the Method are five keys to resolving karma and each key unlocks the door of the self and allows you to sense your own predictions about your life. When put in action these five keys will help you unearth memories that have been buried for years and sometimes for lifetimes.

As a metaphysical intuitive I can guide you back to the place of deepest memory to help you get unstuck, but on your own you can also do a lot of the work. The Karmic Resolution Method will set you on your own path so you can begin to understand your life's journey and read the signposts ahead which will eventually become more visible, even without the aid of a psychic guide. The five keys, however, will give you a good sense of why the Karmic Resolution Method works.

KEY 1: Acknowledging the Problem

The first key to resolving karma is acknowledging the problem and this can only be done through self-awareness. I help my clients by revealing things to them at a higher level of perception, by giving them a broader, objective perspective of their lives. So often we are too close to our own problems or our own behavior patterns or habits to evaluate them properly. Our problem may be obvious to everyone we know except ourselves.

In Alcoholics Anonymous the first thing alcoholics must do to stop drinking and start healing is acknowledge that they have a drinking problem. If they refuse to see their drinking as a problem, they won't be motivated to do anything about it. Until they can stand up and admit their problem, they will remain stuck. This is true of any karmic issue that needs to be resolved. If you walk around wondering why the world is treating you so badly and don't acknowledge your own contributions to your problems, you will never heal.

KEY 2: Understanding the Coincidences

One of the ways that we can develop self-awareness and come to acknowledge our problems is by "putting two and two together" or understanding the coincidences in our lives. As I discussed in the last chapter, what you may think of as a coincidence is actually a message you should pay attention to. It's the Invisible World's way of telling you to wake up and pay attention.

KEY 3: Recognizing the Patterns in Your Life

Once you've acknowledged a problem and added up what you thought were "coincidences" you will start to recognize patterns, if you look closely. A pattern is when you find yourself doing the same things, making the same mistakes, over and over again. You can't break a pattern until you've identified it and acknowledged it.

KEY 4: Opening Up Past and Future Possibilities

When you look at the patterns in your life, the patterns that seem to repeat themselves over and over again, you may feel discouraged. You may think to yourself, "This is just the way I am; there's no way to change it." You may feel as though these negative patterns are just a vicious circle. But they're not—they can be broken. This may be a pattern of failed relationships, or of getting fired from your jobs, or not getting along with certain types of people, or even negative mood patterns. The first thing you need to do is look at the past and see where and when these patterns started to emerge. What are the roots to these patterns? They may just be a behavior that you created as a child that is no longer serving you as an adult. When you open up the past you can learn many things about yourself, but you must be painfully honest.

Once the past has been opened up, the present makes a lot more sense and then the future becomes open to very different possibilities. If you look toward the future and see the same patterns of the past repeating themselves, you will remain stuck. Break linear time in your own mind—picture your life like a lifeline with a past, present, and future and look at them all side by side. If the patterns of the past have not served you well, you must create a turning point. Break the pattern in the present and then you can alter, and even predict, the future. The best way to create a bright future is to have a powerful vision for it. Lay out the vision of the future the way you want it, do the work to eliminate the negative patterns of the past, and put the wheels in motion to make that future reality. That's how you break linear time in your own life. Create a vision, hold on to that vision at all times, and put all your efforts toward that vision and soon that future will be the present reality.

KEY 5: Becoming Aware of Synchronicities

Once your vision for the future is clear and your negative patterns of the past are in the process of being broken, you will find that the energy of the universe will begin to align with your vision. The power of your vision will actually change the energy in your energy field and things will begin to happen the way you want them to. As I said before, everything in the physical world is an illusion, and it is up to you to decide what kind of illusion you want it to be. Synchronicity is the Invisible World's way of letting you know you're on the right path.

Although understanding the Five Keys to Healing is a good start to resolving your karma, before you can move on to the Karmic Resolution Method you must first have a solid understanding of where you are in your spiritual evolution. The only way to do this is to examine your spiritual code and to be aware of the two things that are creating much of your negative karma and preventing you from healing it and moving forward in your life.

CHAPTER FOUR

Accessing Your Spiritual Code

When I was a little girl my father, Victor, always impressed me with his ability to be calm and loving, even in the middle of stressful and chaotic situations. As you can imagine, I wasn't an easy child to raise. Not only was I predicting events before they were happening and jumping up onstage to sing during family vacations, I also started my singing career at a young age and my schedule and the traveling were demanding on my family. Both of my parents were extremely loving and supportive, even if they didn't always understand what was happening with me while it was happening. It was easy to take that love and support for granted, but I realize, now that I'm a mother and now that I see how so many of my clients treat their children, how much spiritual strength that can take. I learned from my own parents what it means to be spiritually evolved.

"The Star That Cries the Most, Shines the Most"

My father had two sayings he used all the time that always stayed with me and taught me some very valuable lessons. He would say, "Carmen, the world is algebra; life is just a series of pluses and minuses." How true! It's all part of the circle of life. We have ups, we have downs, we have gains and we have losses. Handling both our gains and our losses with equanimity is a strong sign of a spiritually evolved person. My father, no doubt, learned this lesson from his own mother, my grandmother, who lived to be 102 years old and was one of the most peaceful people I've ever known. She was in a permanent state of contentment; nothing upset her. When the Communists took her land from her family she said, "Take it." She buried every member of her family saying, "There are not enough tears for the deep wounds of losing someone you love but we build the miracle of life through pain and suffering. God gives, God takes away, he knows, he has a bigger plan."

I've always thought that my grandmother's ability to maintain a sense of inner peace despite her suffering was the reason that she lived so long. She must have learned it from her mother, who had lived to be 112!

The second saying my father used was, "The star that cries the most, shines the most." He thought of each person's spirit like a little star and the spirit who shed cleansing tears would shine brighter. The spirit that goes through pain and suffering will reach Nirvana, reach the good in themselves because they go through the test of pain and out of their pain comes wisdom and self-awareness.

Suffering forces us to go deep into ourselves and to seek out solace from the divine part of us. The key, however, is not to allow suffering to make you bitter or cynical. All suffering is an invitation from God for us to evolve spiritually, to develop self-awareness and deeper levels of perception, and to come to understand our karma.

Every second of our lives we are learning how to heal and free ourselves from our karma. Releasing ourselves from karma is the only way to reach eternity. I've really come to think of everything that you understand as joy and what you don't understand as suffering. When we suffer we are forced to be introspective and to learn from our problems. We gain wisdom and learn lessons.

Your Spiritual Code

I learned from my grandfather that the only way to heal your karma is through knowledge, by identifying or diagnosing your karma and then taking the steps required to turn it around. The first step in diagnosing your karma is accessing your code, or your level of soul evolution.

Every person has a code, where all of our information is stored, and it reveals our individual level of perception and soul evolution. Some people are more evolved than others because they've had more lifetimes to work out their karma or because they have stronger levels of self-awareness and self-understanding. We are all familiar with Darwin's law of evolution, the idea that as a species we shed traits that don't serve us, that prevent us from surviving. It's not just our physical bodies or our levels of intelligence that evolve; our souls also evolve, over each lifetime and over cumulative lifetimes.

Accessing your spiritual code means getting in touch with your essential wisdom by recognizing your authentic self. It is tapping into your deeper spiritual existence. We all have a desperate need to find out who we are, and yet too often we remain blindsided, misguided, or oblivious to our higher selves and we have a tremendous amount of confusion as a result. Accessing your code means finding your true identity. When our lives are in conflict with our true nature, we find suffering at every turn. The artist trapped inside the body of a business executive will eventually self-destruct. It is only when we access our spiritual code that we can find our way back and resolve painful karmic conflicts.

In Chapter One I discussed the fact that as a species, as a society, we are evolving from a place of "I believe" to a place of "I know." This is true of us not just as a species, but as individuals. This means that instead of just believing in the divine within us we come to know the divine within us. Rather than only believing in our infinite potential, we come to know our infinite potential. When we access our code we come to know our true selves and in coming to know our true selves we come to know many other things about our lives. We recognize the path of our lives where we've been in the past, where we are in the present, and where we can go in the future. We come to know our true gifts, skills, and talents. We come to know why certain people are in our lives. We come to know what in our lives needs improving or further exploration. We come to understand our bodies and our health more. We come to know how far we've evolved emotionally and mentally.

So many people I see, however, doubt that they can ever come to know these things about themselves and as a result they make a lot of mistakes in their lives. I can't tell you how many times I hear, "Who cares, I'm going to die anyway." What a pathetic way to refuse to accept responsibility for your own life and your own happiness! It is that type of attitude that allows you to make mistakes that will accumulate and come to haunt you later in this life and others.

I often ask myself, why do people do this to themselves? Why don't they operate at their full potential and know themselves well enough to make the right choices? I think they are afraid to "know." Of course many people's greatest fear is the unknown, which is exactly why I say, come to know the unknown, come to a place of knowledge. Once you have knowledge there is no longer anything to be afraid of.

Working with people for many years has helped me acknowledge that there are very easy ways to access our true identity. We don't see ourselves; we are not aware of who we are; we can't see ourselves from the inside out and realize that the image we see in the mirror is irrelevant. What we see in the mirror is insufficient to sum up who we are. We are often confused by appearances, by what we see on the surface, and it takes true wisdom to go beneath it, with oneself and in relationships with others.

When I see people for the first time I tap into their true selves. I access their code to see where they are in their soul evolution, how deep their level of perception is. Some psychics call this doing a "reading" but I call it "accessing the code" or "decoding the data." If the data is accessible to us, we will always know what we have to do next and what challenges we will be facing next. If we know how to tap into someone else's code we can anticipate events and behavior patterns. However, the code is quite sophisticated. The memory of the data isn't "awake," the subconscious isn't always in touch with the conscious mind. That is why we can often seem "asleep" in our own lives, why we do things without awareness or attribute things to fate when in fact we subconsciously made a choice. We think fate is something we can't control, that it's something beyond us, when in fact it is within us.

There are two different types of people: the believers and the skeptics. There are those who want to know and move forward and those who cling to the old, who are stuck, who don't want to know. There are a lot of skeptics who come to me, and I recognize it right away. They don't want to see themselves and they don't want anyone else to see them, either. I think they are afraid. They are unhappy, and they've been unhappy through many lives. Perhaps they are afraid to bring that sadness out into the open; they are afraid to face their own unhappiness and their own role in it. They prefer to perceive the world around them through a narrow lens, through their own weaknesses, through their emotions, rather than through the truth. I also see a lot of people who are open and they always walk in with a big smile on their faces. They may be suffering, they may be confused, but they know that they don't know and they are willing and eager to learn more and so they do.

Two Sets of Laws

As I've already said, there is the world of the physical, the Visible World, the walking world of human beings, and then there is the Invisible World. Each of these worlds has its own set of laws, and they are quite different. The Visible World operates at the level of human laws and the Invisible World operates at the level of the Universal Laws. You are already familiar with the human laws because you are living with them right now. They are limiting and meant to control and contain. The Universal Laws, on the other hand, reveal a world of infinite possibility. People who understand and live by the Universal Laws are more spiritually evolved.

Human beings have been aware of this for many centuries and their stories and myths reflect the need to understand the difference between the two levels of existence. In the East there are many stories of gods and goddesses and the various things they do to reach Nirvana. In the West there is the story of Adam and Eve and original sin. Originally man and woman lived in an earthly paradise and were immortal. It was only through negative action that they lost their paradise and were made to suffer. In Latin the word "sin" means disconnect. Sin is the disconnection between the visible and the invisible, the disparity between the human laws and the Universal Laws. When Jesus said, "I want to take sin away," he meant that he wanted to re-create the connection between man and the divine.

God said the world is perfectly harmonious and peaceful but the world we live in today is anything but harmonious and peaceful. This isn't God's fault, this is man's fault. We left the peace and harmony of the Universal Laws in favor of our man-made laws which are driven by our egos and our emotions. We must live with the knowledge that beyond the physical law there is another element; there is a divine intelligence. The purpose of our lives in the physical world is to learn about the spiritual world and develop a constant communication with God through our thoughts, deeds, and words, and to come to know the higher spiritual intelligence of the Invisible World. It's all an effort to repair the disconnection between the visible and the invisible.

As we make the transition from "I believe" to "I know," we will be able to solve the problems of mankind and to reveal the light from the darkness. Even though we've moved forward technologically and are advanced in the physical world, we are lost in the mind, the soul, the internal world. We have moved farther and farther away from the divine which is why we are so confused and unhappy. Negative energy is contagious and when we absorb it or create it, it takes away our potential for happiness and it damages our health. Evolution is peace. Evolution is understanding and wisdom. It is knowing how to solve our problems, how to have harmony in our relationships, knowing our life purpose, knowing our reason for being here.

Evolution is when we change into different forms in

accordance with the memory we create. Every day you plan conscious actions. Negative thoughts, actions, and emotions stem from living in the ego, and living in the ego creates negative karma. Everything you do comes back to you. Karmically this negativity will come back to haunt you. If you create good, you free yourself from the wheel of negativity, but as long as your thoughts, actions, and emotions are negative, you will remain in darkness.

A Battle Between Two Selves

The disconnection between the Visible and Invisible worlds is something that we experience most intensely in the ongoing battle between our personality/ego and our true self/soul. This conflict shows up every day, but we must do the work required to repair the rift.

Your personality is confronted with your soul, and the level of soul evolution you have reached. The more evolved you are spiritually, the less the conflict will be between your soul and your personality. When you can bridge these two aspects of your self, you will be more peaceful and happy.

You have to do your own work to discover who you really are. What are your needs? What are you searching for? Why is this person in your life? What is the purpose of your soul? You have to realize that nothing in your life is an accident; everything happens as a way to help you find your purpose. We are all so needy when it comes to identifying ourselves and usually we rely on the opinions of others rather than going within. We seem almost incapable of creating a true self-identity and we can create a tremendous amount of confusion as a result.

So many people don't know who they are or where they are in their lives so the timing of their choices is "off." So much of being happy in life is about timing. The timing has to be right for certain things to happen. Someone with a higher level of perception can see what needs to be done and when, how to make things happen when the timing is right.

Several years ago, a famous model came to see me for the first time. I'll call her Angela. As soon as she sat down I said to her, "You're pregnant." She looked at me with complete surprise and said defiantly, "Nobody knows I'm pregnant. I just found out yesterday. I don't understand how you can know this, but I'm not going to have the baby anyway. I'm not married and it would ruin my career."

I looked at her and said, "You came to me for a reason. This baby is a major event that will change your life for the better. You will keep the baby; it's part of your destiny."

Seven months later I saw her on television. She was pregnant and talking about how happy she was to be having the baby. She was beaming. She has since had the baby and is happily married. Her ego told her she couldn't have the baby—the fact that she wasn't married and was at the peak of her modeling career made her think having a baby was impossible.

We all have these two elements to our being: the ego/personality and the true self/soul. There needs to be a strong connection and communication between the two elements. Typically we see ourselves in a very limited way—purely at the first level, at the level of the ego or personality. We don't know how to bridge the levels to our own advantage. Angela, whose beauty was such a central part of her identity as well as her career, felt threatened by becoming pregnant; her ego felt threatened. But at the level of her soul, she knew she wanted to have the baby. When she came to me she wanted to find out what the next step in her life was. Her conscious mind didn't want to acknowledge that motherhood was her next step, but her superconscious mind knew better. There is always a higher level within you that you must get in touch with before you make any decisions in your life. Angela's ego tried to make a decision at first, but ultimately she made her decision at the soul level.

The soul has other needs beyond those of the ego. The soul wants to resolve karma, to do good, to resolve the problems that the ego causes. The soul carries the memory and the spiritual life; it carries the beautiful part of you. The soul has no need for money or sex or other needs of the body. When we die we let go of all these needs and transform into pure love. And we forgive and ask for forgiveness.

When I say forgive I mean it in a broader sense than perhaps you are used to. Forgive is a Greek word that means "to detach." Never in life should we get too attached to anything, not to material things, not to people, or even to ideas. Anything that you get too attached to, whether it be a person, a certain financial energy, a career, a house, an object, will become destructive, or it will control you. Losing this thing becomes unbearable and usually, when you reach that point you do lose it. That loss is one of the greatest opportunities you may be given to learn and evolve.

The only attachment we should have is to God, to the divine universe. We come alone into this world and we leave it alone. We can get love and support from others, from our parents, our children, our spouse or lover, our friends, but ultimately wisdom and spiritual resilience and soul evolution come from within ourselves.

One of my clients, Jennifer, lived alone for a long time. She had a bad relationship with her parents; she didn't have any friends; she just had two dogs who were her constant companions and her only relationship. Every time she came to me she would say, "If my dogs ever die, I will die." She felt that her dogs were the only things she had, the only thing she had to live for.

I am a big animal lover and I have an adorable dog and a cat myself and I love them very much, but I knew that Jennifer was using her dogs to avoid evolving and learning how to develop relationships with other people. I explained to her over and over that she had to find another meaning in her life; she couldn't get so attached to the dogs because the moment we get that deeply attached to something or someone, we will lose it.

Two years after she started coming to me, one of her dogs died from cancer. Jennifer had been hysterical when he was diagnosed, begging me to save his life. I had a vision of a doctor upstate who could help her and indeed she found the doctor and that doctor prolonged the dog's life for eight more months. But in the end the dog did die. And three days later she came home and found the second dog dead in the house. She was inconsolable, hysterical, angry, and incapable of understanding how this could happen. She remembered what I told her, that whatever we become too attached to, we lose. She took this crisis and her grief as an opportunity to examine her life, to find her self, and to build other relationships despite the hurt she had suffered from her parents. She could have easily allowed herself to wallow in her despair, to be full of self-pity or to become angry and bitter. But she didn't. Under my guidance, and with the Karmic Resolution Method, she came to understand how to fulfill the needs of her soul. And she learned forgiveness and detachment. And she eventually reunited with her parents.

Jennifer's lesson can be applied to many other situations. Many people become so attached to their work or making money that they ignore the other people around them, or they use it as a way to avoid facing themselves at a deeper level. When they lose that job or lose their money they are devastated and have an identity crisis. Without these things they no longer know who they are! Loss of physical things is difficult, but it is an opportunity to get in touch with the needs of your soul, to go beyond the ego into the better part of yourself.

We always want somebody or something else to save us or to be there for us or to gratify us, but ultimately we all have to learn to access our deeper self and develop our own spiritual strength.

The Ego and the Emotional System

There are two powerful reasons why we have such a difficult time coming to know our true self-identity—the ego and the emotions—and they are at the root of most of our problems. Once you leave the physical you no longer have emotions; you no longer have an ego; you are only your soul. People who die and go into the Invisible World aren't angry; they aren't bitter; they aren't sad. They live in a constant state of love; they ask for forgiveness for the wrong they did in the physical world. Even the souls that were bad in the physical world live in this state. As long as you're here and have ego problems and negative emotions you will be unhappy.

The Emotional System

Every experience you've had resurfaces as an emotion during your lifetime and this emotion will play itself out in seemingly unrelated situations again and again. Every single negative thought or experience will resurface in the emotions and develop into a behavior pattern. A lot of the time our emotions are a result of having to confront things that we fear. If we are afraid of the dark, afraid of commitment, afraid of water, afraid of being revealed, when we are confronted with that situation we will express it through anger, jealousy, hatred, blame, and frustration. Sometimes we call this "pushing our buttons." If you are in balance you can control the emotions. If you are out of balance the emotions will control you and define who you are.

Life is an endless process of learning how to deal with our emotional system. Our emotions are the way we project the world from the inside to the world outside. But if our emotions aren't in our control they can send the wrong message to the outside world and they can mask our true self.

The emotional system is a purely physical phenomenon; in the spirit world, in the Invisible World, there are no emotions, there is only peace. It is easy to mistake the emotions we feel as our true identity. We have free will and it is up to us to move forward, to move toward perfection and to stop being slaves to our emotions.

People who are angry will attract more anger; people who are negative will attract more negativity; the karma is amplified and what you feel is what you attract. People who are more spiritually evolved have an easier time with the emotional system. They are more at peace; they don't get as angry, as jealous, and they aren't as negative.

The way to deal with your emotions is to acknowledge that you have them, recognize them for what they are, and try to find the source of the emotion. If you are jealous of another person and you deny that you are, you will just continue to be jealous, contributing to your own unhappiness. The day you acknowledge that you are jealous, you can begin to heal. You can admit to yourself that you have a problem with jealousy; you can try to examine the reason behind the jealousy and then, armed with that deeper level of awareness, you can disarm it and let it fall away. You can't break a pattern if you don't understand that the problem is in you, at the level of your emotions. You need to acknowledge it and then let the emotion go. Walk away; release it; make peace with it. Only then is the karma resolved.

The Ego

People who live by their egos look at life pragmatically; and they tend to live by the human laws. Even if they go to church or synagogue, it is more for a human tradition than grounded in any real spiritual basis. They truly believe that there is nothing more to life than human existence, which to me seems very sad and limiting. I can't imagine going through life with such a small view of existence and life's purpose, of never seeing anything other than what is here on earth.

The ego believes that physical existence is all that there is and so it becomes consumed with possessions, bank accounts, homes, achievement, appearances, status, sexual and physical needs. If the needs of the ego are not met, the emotions run wild. I've had so many clients say, "Why is God doing this to me?" or "I hate God, he isn't helping me; he doesn't exist." They don't realize that it is their own egos causing their problems. They should be asking, "Why is my ego doing this to me?" or "I hate my ego, it isn't helping me."

People who live in their egos look at the world materialistically; they are skeptical; they live very much down on the ground, what they would call, "down to earth." They will say that they look at life pragmatically, they are being "realistic" but they are less connected to a higher self and ultimately, are less evolved. In their arrogance they will rarely look at themselves honestly or ask for forgiveness. Only when they go through a traumatic event—death, illness, or loss—do they see something beyond their limited reality, as in Jennifer's case. It takes a dramatic life event for them to acknowledge that they have a soul, to accept that their own limited perception is the root of their bad karma.

I'll never forget Mark, a client whose jealousy was constantly getting in his own way. No matter what he had, it wasn't good enough. Somebody else always had something better. When a coworker got a big promotion he reacted with anger. "I scored the last big account, why did he get the promotion?" When his best friend fell in love he refused to acknowledge the girlfriend and didn't try to build a relationship with her. Rather than enjoying the fact that his best friend was deliriously happy, he could only focus on the fact that his best friend was no longer as available to him. He wrote it off, whining, "He's only in it for the sex. And now I'm losing my best friend."

Mark couldn't understand that his own negativity was at the root of his problems; it was why he didn't get the promotion and why his friend began to withdraw. This negativity became a part of who he was; it was how people began to perceive him. He got stuck in a downward cycle, never feeling as though he was getting what he wanted, and he was becoming bitter. It was hard for Mark to learn that negativity attracts more negativity.

Like Mark we all project from the inside out. Everything in the physical world is an illusion and it is up to us to decide what kind of illusion it will be. The ego and the emotional system are part of that illusion and will cause you great pain if you allow these to control you. When you begin to access your spiritual code, you will connect to your soul and seeing the disparity between your outward personality and your soul will be painful at first. But it will allow you to change the way you live, to live from the place of the soul. Because what matters in the end is not the way we look or how much we can accumulate or the wealth we generate. What matters is accessing the freedom and peace of your soul that I call wisdom, which is gained through self-awareness and by living by the Universal Laws.

Living by the Universal Laws

People who have accessed their spiritual code are more evolved, have learned more of life's lessons, have more self-understanding, and higher levels of perception. They are wiser, they have a level of maturity, harmony, and perfection in their thoughts and actions. They spend their lives trying to create peace; they have re-connected to the divine part of themselves and live accordingly. These people are aware of the Universal Laws, which help in spiritual growth and help the soul reach Nirvana, immortality, and release from karma.

I first learned about the Universal Laws from my grandfather and they are the underlying principles of this book and of my work. They are, in a way, a guide on how to live. The Universal Laws are designed to help you strive toward perfection and to connect to the Universal intelligence. If you operate within these laws you will have a harmonious life. If you operate outside of them, you will create unbalance and suffering for yourself. There are many Universal Laws but I will focus on the ones I think are most important.

1. The Law of Karma: This is the most important law. The purpose of this law is to help you attain harmony and balance in your life. Through your intentions, thoughts, emotions, words, and deeds you create karma. In order to live in perfect harmony you must resolve your karma. You have to decide on your own what you need to learn in order to resolve your karma and where your karma is. My Karmic Resolution Method in the final chapter of this book will help you begin to do that.

2. The Law of Wisdom: Wisdom is knowing what you have the power to change and what you don't. It is using your suffering as a way to learn about yourself. You will experience less pain in your life, learn your lessons more peacefully, and prevent and resolve your problems more readily once you gain wisdom. Through wisdom and patience every karmic issue can be resolved.

3. The Law of Evolution: The only way to gain wisdom is by spiritually evolving. We all need to rise above our emotions and egos and evolve in the direction of our souls. Usually this is done through many failures and mistakes. If you don't learn from your failures and mistakes; if you don't strive toward the direction of your soul and away from your ego and emotions, you will live in darkness and suffering.

4. The Law of Vibrational Energy: We are all energy that is constantly moving and the spirit that lives within us as energy never dies. Nothing in the universe is fixed; everything is constantly transforming, and that includes us and our lives.

5. The Law of Oneness: We have a collective awareness and consciousness and all of us are influenced by one another. We are all part of the greater whole.

6. The Law of Love: We are here to love one another, not to hate, not to kill. Love is the answer to everything; it is the most important element to every healing process. People have become very confused about what love is—there is only one real love: unconditional love. With unconditional love you heal yourself and others.

7. The Law of Abundance: The Universe was designed so that each person would have all that they need. Unfortunately greed has created outsized needs and has created an imbalance in the world and many people exist in a place of scarcity instead of abundance. We are all meant to live in a state of abundance and enjoy all that we need without limits. Abundance is not just about having "things," it is about having happiness, and joy, and coming to know ourselves and relishing life.

8. The Law of Divine Order: There is a divine order in the universe, a divine plan. Everything is planned and in divine control, although it may not always appear that way. If we live by the divine order instead of by man-made laws, we will live in the abundance of the divine. God knows better; what may appear to be a loss today may be a gain tomorrow. Learn to say, "Let go and let God" when things aren't working out as you would like. Put your trust in the divine order.

9. The Law of Gratitude: An important part of our evolution is learning to be grateful for all that we have, something most of us don't do. Don't take anything for granted; be grateful for every wonderful thing, big or small, that's in your life.

10. The Law of Harmony: The universe is meant to be in perfect harmony and peace. If we don't see it this

way and feel that the universe is chaotic, if we don't acknowledge its perfection, we are doomed to live our
lives in a state of fear and to cause the very chaos our
minds have created. Respecting the innate harmony of
the universe means living by the Universal Laws; it
means not to kill, lie, hate, or steal. It means to live from
a place of love and the divine.

11. The Law of Manifestation: Everything you think
will manifest into reality. Three hundred years ago the
philosopher Descartes said, "I think, therefore I am."
The way we think creates our reality. Thinking transforms into deeds and our deeds become who we are.

12. The Law of Detachment: We are only here on earth
for a limited time so we should not get too attached to
any material thing or physical person. Strong attachments create an imbalance in the energy and you will live
from your emotions or your ego. The only way to remain
in balance is to be in perfect connection with the divine.

13. The Law of Attitude: Although you can't control
everything that happens to you, you can control how
you respond; you can control your attitude. Nothing
can hurt you as much as your own negative attitude.
The way you treat yourself and others and the situations
in your life create karma.

14. The Law of Acceptance: Whatever you resist will
make you suffer. Resistance is fear; acceptance is harmony. Don't try to change what you can't. And often,
what you resist, you become.

15. The Law of Duality: There are two forces at work
in the universe, yin and yang, male and female energy,

and we need both of them to live in harmony. There is also good and evil, harmony and chaos—there is always a tension, of opposites tugging at each other. The key is not to let the tension become destructive; don't allow negative forces and tension to throw you off balance.

16. The Law of Trinity: Each of us is made up of three elements: the body, mind, and spirit. The physical body is controlled by the ego; the mind is controlled by the intellect; and the spirit is controlled by the soul. The pyramid is an example of the Law of Trinity—it has three points and is a symbol of stability. The three parts of the trinity must work in unison and harmony.

17. The Law of Attraction: What you are, you will attract. If you are negative, like Mark, you will attract more negativity. If you are afraid of something, it will show up in your life, so you must eliminate the fear. The lessons you are meant to learn will show up, you will attract them. The way to attract the good, is to be good. The way to attract love, is to be love.

18. The Law of Divinity: Everyone of us has divinity within us. When we become aware that we are divine, we can begin to act in a way that reflects that divinity.

19. The Law of Cycles: All of our lives are made up of different cycles. When you complete one cycle, another one will begin. Typically cycles last nine to twelve years and there are four or five major cycles of your life. Be aware of where you are, in which cycle. Major events like marriage, the death of a parent, or the birth of a child are parts of cycles and create turning points to help you reach a new level of awareness.

20. The Law of Destiny: Destiny is what you are here to experience; it is the sum of your life experiences and the lessons you learn along the way. We each have our own destiny and we are meant to fulfill it.

21. The Law of Dharma: In Hinduism and Buddhism they use the word "dharma" to mean the ultimate order of all things. It means nothing more than that an individual's conduct should be in alignment with the Universal Laws, the divine order. This is our ultimate mission: to align ourselves with the divine. Dharma and karma work hand in hand. Our karma will be affected to the extent that we live according to dharma.

*H*ow many of us live each day so that our thoughts and actions reflect the purest intentions of our souls? God knows, and I mean God really knows, that none of us is perfect. However, perfection exists in the Invisible World, and it is our souls' purpose to forever strive toward that perfection. When we live strictly by human laws we suffer; when we live by the Universal Laws we heal our karma. In Part II I will explore ways to resolve your karma in three important areas of your life: your relationships, your health, and in fulfilling your life purpose.

LIVING IN THE VISIBLE WORLD: A WEB OF INFINITE POSSIBILITIES

CHAPTER FIVE

Creating Karmic Relationships

Almost every person who comes to me is in search of insight into his or her romantic life. For many, many people it is extremely difficult to find the right person—someone they can love unconditionally and who will love them in return, and who will make them feel fulfilled and complete. Whenever I do private readings or conduct seminars, I'm always asked, "Will I be in a relationship soon?" "Is the person I'm dating 'the one'?" "Why do I always end up with the same type of person?" or "Why don't my relationships ever work out?"

Nowhere in our lives is our emotional system and our ego tested more than in our relationships with other people. Our ability to give and receive love is crucial for healing and spiritual growth, whether it be with a spouse, lover, parent, child, or friend, and yet we find it so difficult to do! Some of our relationships are "in tune" karmically and others aren't. Some work and some are extremely difficult. So why is this, and how can we all attract more harmonious relationships?

Sometimes people think they've found each other and they're ecstatically happy, everything is just perfect. Then a year or two later, they begin to face difficulties, and they feel like they've been deceived. They thought they knew their lovers but found out that their lovers weren't who they thought they were, and their lovers weren't able to live up to their expectations. This happens so often; I see this all the time; and it is usually at this crucial moment that people decide to break up or divorce.

So much of this pain could be alleviated if we simply examined ourselves, our expectations, and what we want in a mate, before we let our emotions take over, get "swept away" and decide to get married. For example, one of my clients, Daphne, first came to me when she was in her early thirties. She was tall and thin, with long blond hair, a high paying prestigious job, and a terrific sense of humor and strong wit. Her entire life men had pursued her, and while she dated regularly, she never really cared for any of them and, on the surface at least, remained cynical about marriage and relationships.

What Daphne didn't usually tell people was that her father was an alcoholic and although he was never physically abusive, he was emotionally absent. A successful man, he went to work every day and provided financially for his family, but when Daphne was growing up she never received the love and validation she desperately craved. She focused on her looks, developed her wit, and created a reputation as a fun-loving party girl to gain the attention of other men. She became something of a "prize" with many men vying for her attention but she never felt loved for herself.

She first came to me to find out when she would get married. Many of her peers were getting married and she secretly started to panic, thinking if she got any older she would no longer be able to find a "rich, good-looking" husband; she felt she was rapidly approaching her "expiration date."

One night at a party she met Brad, a tall, handsome man, with a degree from a prestigious school, who could match her wit. On their first date he said, "You're going to be my wife" and she fell under his spell. Here, finally, was a man who had all the qualities she thought she wanted. So when Brad began to tell her negative things about her friends' loyalty or behavior she never questioned him and instead, stopped socializing with her girlfriends. She began to spend all of her time with him, dropping her other interests, and within a year they got married.

Throughout the entire wedding planning process she was ecstatically happy, but things started to go wrong as soon as they were on their honeymoon. Now that she was his wife, Brad didn't want Daphne to go anywhere without him, and he didn't want other men looking at her. He became incredibly jealous and they began to argue. Unfortunately she had dropped most of her friends so she had no one to turn to as Brad's jealousy became more and more pronounced. She, in turn, became equally jealous, jealous of any time he spent away from her. They wouldn't allow each other to spend any time apart, but in all the time they spent together they argued constantly, accusing each other of imagined infidelities and unloving behavior. Within six months they had separated and within one year they were divorced, and all of Daphne's dreams were shattered.

Because of her own unexamined fears and expectations, Daphne wasn't able to read the signs Brad had been sending about his jealousy and insecurities. And she had never resolved her own karma with her father, so she wasn't ready to have a true relationship. Neither one of them was evolved enough to have a mature relationship or to bring out the best in each other, or to get beyond the superficial to let true love develop.

In order to create a stable relationship we must work hard to resolve our karma because in an intimate relationship, more than anywhere else, all of our past karma, all of our issues, come back to haunt us: our problems with our parents, our career frustrations, our deepest fears and expectations, the pain of our past relationships. If we haven't resolved these issues before we enter a relationship they will simply resurface and accumulate and potentially destroy the relationship.

My Own Love Story

In my own life my grandfather provided me with tremendous guidance, so when I first met the man who is now my husband, I was prepared. My grandfather had always told me I would come to the United States and meet a man with a mustache whose name started with a *V*, the same initial as my father Victor, and that I would meet him and marry him right away and stay with him in the United States. I also had other signs and synchronicities along the way that helped me to recognize my husband when I first met him.

In 1983, I came here for a concert and a man who had heard me sing called me and asked if I would sing in his restaurant. I said, "Sure, I'll come by and meet with you" and when I showed up at the restaurant a handsome man with a mustache walked out and introduced himself as Virgil. I freaked out because I knew immediately that he was the man my grandfather had been telling me about!

When we met we both felt that we knew each other extremely well; we both had a feeling of déjà vu. Though we were seeing each other for the first time, we felt we had known each other before. Karmically, we both knew it was right. He asked me to marry him three weeks after we met and we've been married ever since. He and I were familiar with each other; we were a part of each other's memory. It was an instant attraction and connection. It wasn't the first time I had been in love. Years before, I had been in love with a producer in Romania, but this time, I knew it was the real thing.

You often hear of love at first sight or people who meet and recognize each other and while it sounds incredible, it can happen. We need to learn how to trust our "knowing." We also need to recognize that there is something in us that will tell us if this is the right person. And we can do this only if we have already worked on our own evolution, on accessing our code. You will never find your soul mate if you can't recognize him or her.

Finding Your Soul Mate

Before you can find a soul mate, you should understand what a soul mate really is. As I described earlier, all of life is a circle and energy flows and transforms throughout that circle. The theme of the circle is also true in our relationships. Each of us is half a sphere and the only way to complete the sphere is through an intimate relationship with another person. I'm sure you've heard the phrase, "She or he is my better half." We are each halves of a whole and our soul mate is our destined other half. To feel fulfilled and alive, to learn some of your greatest karmic lessons, is to have a relationship with another person who melds exactly into your circle, who has the same level of karmic energy, and helps the energy flow within you. The energy of the two halves merge together and have more room to flow; the energy mingles and each of you is given the opportunity to evolve and grow.

Finding your soul mate can be a long process. Some people do it at a young age, but for others it can take almost a lifetime. A soul mate is someone with whom you develop a strong affinity because you share the same life purpose. A soul mate is someone who complements you and vice versa. They are a reflection of the things you need to learn, the things that are missing in you. Soul mates are karmically in tune with each other. Within each of us there are pluses and minuses that exist in our souls (our positive energy and qualities and our negative energy and qualities). A soul mate complements and balances the energy you are missing, and you do the same for him or her.

As I've already explained, before you can find a soul mate you must do the work to know yourself better. You must identify your road in life, know who you really are, see the good and bad in yourself honestly, and know what your goals and needs are.

The very moment we meet someone, there is usually a little voice inside of us that tells us if this person is someone we can trust, feel safe with, and connect with. Unfortunately, when it comes to romantic love, the voice of our body chemistry or our emotions is usually much louder and more urgent and it may drown our inner voice out. If you are serious about finding a soul mate you need to learn to hear your inner voice, and listen to the messages it is telling you, rather than letting the ego or the emotions get in the way.

The ego and emotions intervene by focusing on the wrong things, as Daphne did, and thinking this is "true love." It could mean you think your physical attraction to someone else, the allure of their looks, their money, or what they can "do for you" is true love. These external benefits can tempt you to get involved with someone who, beneath all of their external attractiveness, isn't right for you karmically.

One of the biggest problems in relationships today is that people let these irrelevant external factors, not their inner voice, guide their romantic lives and their choice of a partner. But you should never marry or date somebody's success. You should never marry or date somebody's money. You should never marry or date someone based on physical or sexual chemistry. You should never marry or date somebody's family. You should never marry or date somebody's past. You should never marry or date somebody based solely on their looks.

Joanna is a good example. When I met her she was a twenty-six-year-old woman working in a restaurant and struggling to make ends meet. Not long after coming to me, she met a rich man who was a few years older than she. He helped her with her bills, took her on generous shopping sprees, and even took her to Paris on the Concorde for a long weekend. No man had ever treated her so well! She was head over heels for him and convinced that he was the soul mate she'd been waiting for. I sensed that he was wrong for her and told her so, but she would soon learn that for herself.

Several months after they'd started dating he confessed to her that he was married, that his wife was pregnant, and that he couldn't see her anymore. She was shocked and devastated, but she could have avoided a lot of the pain she suffered if she had listened to that inner voice that told her she was being seduced by his money, not by him. Her evolved self always knew this but she didn't pay attention. Instead, her fears about her shaky financial situation prevented her from seeing the obvious red lights in the relationship. She didn't look at the relationship deeply; she just allowed herself to be swept away because she so desperately wanted it to be right.

On the other hand, external factors can also prevent you from pursuing a relationship with someone who may not fit your ideal of "attractiveness" but may ultimately be your true soul mate. For example, both men and women come to see me with an entire laundry list of what they want in a soul mate but the qualities on this list give me great concern. They won't date or marry someone who doesn't make a certain amount of money, who doesn't dress well, who didn't grow up in the right part of town, who is a different religion, who is divorced, or who has children from a previous relationship or who is younger or older than a certain age or . . . you get the picture. The list of "don'ts" goes on and on. They don't show up with these lists on a piece of paper but once I investigate their relationship patterns and hear more about whom they have dated or married or been involved with, it becomes clear that their perception of a soul mate is extremely limited.

For example, my client Rachel didn't understand why she couldn't find the right man to marry. She had been going on two or three blind dates every week for almost two years and just by virtue of playing the odds, she felt she should have clicked with someone by now. She felt she had dated every "eligible" man in town and was afraid she would run out of prospects soon. These dates were usually arranged by her friends or family members and consisted of introducing her to "appropriate" men. To her family and friends "appropriate" meant a couple of years older, well established with a promising career and good income, from the same religious background, and from a good school. This woman was attractive, intelligent, and had an interesting job, but she rarely made it to a second or third date and complained that she never felt a "spark."

One weekend she went to a party at a coworker's apartment, with a crowd of people she didn't usually hang out with. At this party she met a man she described as extremely cute, witty, and charming, and she felt an immediate connection to him. As a matter of fact, they spent most of the party sitting on the couch together sharing personal stories and forming a bond. The problem, as she saw it, was that he was a couple of years younger and came from a very different background. He even had long hair, which she found sexy but felt it showed he was "irresponsible." She dated him for three months and had never felt more connected to anyone, but she broke it off "before it got too serious" because she felt "he wasn't marriage material." She continued to go on blind dates that led nowhere and couldn't understand why she was so miserable.

Rachel was so focused on external factors, searching for a mate coming from the place of the ego, that when she met someone she actually connected to on a soul level she couldn't recognize it, and even worse, resisted it, because he didn't fulfill her ego's expectations.

So how can you identify whether the person you're with is right for you or how do you recognize them if you're still looking? So many of us do look for love from the place of the ego instead of the place of the true self or soul. How do we know what our true self really wants? The following exercise can help you become more clear.

FINDING YOUR DREAM LOVER: MEDITATION FOR CONJURING YOUR IDEAL SOUL MATE

This exercise is most effective when done as a writing exercise. Find some time alone in a quiet, comfortable place where you won't be interrupted and meditate on the following questions. It's better to first be in the habit of go-ing through the Karmic Resolution Method before doing this exercise because knowing your own karma and true identity is the first step to finding a soul mate.

1. Look in your conscious mind the external or physical reality of your ideal mate. Acknowledge the external qualities that you are attracted to and write them down in a journal. Everyone has an ideal in their mind and will always be attracted to that.

2. Write down how you would like to be treated by this person and how you would want to treat this person in return. Examine the needs of your soul and make a list of the qualities that would satisfy your true self.

3. Now make a list of your past relationships—go ahead and list all of them by name. You may have a short list or a long list, several short relationships or just one long one. This exercise will trigger your memory and will probably create many different feelings in you, some painful, some sad, some happy and sweet. Go ahead and allow yourself to experience those emotions for a short time but don't wallow in them; let them go. Now look at these relationships objectively and acknowledge what wasn't working in each of these relationships, why the relationship didn't last. As you write this, pay attention to your own fears, insecurities, your weaknesses and the emotions—whether they be anger, or jealousy, or spitefulness—that usually got in your way.

4. Now look at the common denominators in these relationships and be aware of what you attract. How in synch were these relationships with the above list of qualities you said you wanted? The discrepancy may be revealing. Perhaps the external, "ego" qualities you like and the "soul" qualities your true self desires have been in

conflict. Reevaluate your list of qualities and think of what is truly important to you. The needs of the soul are far more important than the needs of the ego. That is why we look for a "soul mate" not an "ego mate."

5. Now form a vision in your mind of your ideal soul mate, based on these qualities. Allow this vision to become clear in your mind. Forming a picture of the ideal person is the first step in finding that person. The subconscious mind creates the reality first, then the image will be transmitted onto your conscious mind. Once your mind has created the picture, your every action will turn it into a reality. And you will recognize him or her when you see your soul mate.

6. Open your heart and your soul to unconditional love so you are ready when your soul mate appears.

What's Blocking You?

If you want to be in a relationship but find that you're still alone or that you are in a relationship but still don't feel that you've found the love of your life, it may be that there are negative memories and emotions that are haunting you and preventing you from finding or connecting with your soul mate.

In order to picture someone else in your life, you need to be aware of negative emotions, experiences, and patterns that are embedded in your subconscious and eliminate them! Some people can fixate on negative memories for five, ten, fifteen, or even forty years and this prevents them from finding true love and true happiness. Becoming aware of your negative memories will allow you to let go of the negative vibrations that are preventing you from being in love.

When it comes to love, once you make a mistake the first time it will often repeat itself again and again. For example, you may choose people who cheat on you, or drink too much, who are abusive or uncommunicative. I see this all the time with the people I work with. Ninety-nine percent of the women I see don't know who the right person is and keep choosing the wrong ones over and over, usually with the same disastrous results. They ask, "I'm fifty years old! Why have I divorced three times and find myself alone now?" The more bad karma you attract, the more baggage you have, the more mistakes you make, the more you get stuck in a pattern and can't find your way out.

For example, one of my clients, Marlo, is a lovely woman in her mid-forties who came to me broken-hearted over her relationship with John. She came to me with an achingly familiar refrain. "When will I find true love—I can't go on this way . . . ," she sobbed. She had lived with John for five years and was happier with him than with any other man, yet she was constantly searching for clues of John's infidelity, plagued by insecurity and jealousy. Her suspicions became a self-fulfilling prophecy when she discovered that he had been with another woman on a business trip. Devastated, she confronted him in tears, only to hear that it was her constant suspicion and jealousy that forced him into the arms of another woman.

Where did Marlo's seeds of self-hatred and insecurity come from? I led her through the Five Keys to Healing and had her practice the Karmic Resolution Method, and over time she came to recognize a pattern that began when she was a little girl. Every man, beginning with her own father, had let her down, abandoned her, treated her badly. She came to expect this type of treatment from men and consequently, most of the men in her life were unfaithful or unreliable.

John, on the other hand, was different and was genuinely loyal to Marlo but she expected betrayal and her self-fulfilling prophecy came true. Once she was able to look over the time line of her life and see this recurring pattern, she was able to break the cycle. She improved her self-esteem, and believed that she deserved love and fidelity and was finally able to establish more loving relationships.

Another pattern of bad karma I see over and over again are women and men who get into relationships with people who are married. And I see a lot of married men and women who are having affairs. This is so common I don't know why these people bothered to get married in the first place! They are in conflict with themselves; they know what they are doing is wrong and they do it anyway. This is a karmic mistake that will always have negative consequences, whether it destroys their marriage and their way of life, the lives of their children, or their health.

I counseled a man many years ago who had a beautiful loving wife, a young boy, a beautiful house, and a successful career. He and his wife played tennis every weekend with another couple who lived in their neighborhood. When I saw him I warned him that he would face temptation and that he must resist it and stay faithful to his wife or risk losing everything. I told him to appreciate all he had. Sadly, he didn't take my advice. He had an affair with his neighbor and his own wife threw him out of the house. He lost his home, his wife, his son, and was forced to rent an apartment in town. None of the neighbors would talk to him; his wife wouldn't take him back; his little boy's heart was broken, and within two years the man developed cancer. It was a tragic story; this man was sick, he could no longer work, and there was no one there to take care of him. He created bad karma that accumulated and spread out to every part of his life. I wish I could say there was a happy ending for this story, but there wasn't.

A happier story is Felicia's. I met Felicia when she was twenty-three. She had just left her family in Paris to come to America to build her life. Shortly after arriving here she met a man who was married with three children. He helped her with her career and supported her while she got on her feet, but ultimately, he treated her like a mistress, which is to say, he kept her a secret. She wasn't allowed to call him, and his family always came first. At my advice she left him.

Within a year she met another married man, this one with one child, and she told me, "This is different, he loves me, Carmen; he's going to leave his wife." How many times have I heard that line? I told her that this man was not different, that she was attracting the same energy and creating a pattern that would take a lot of work for her to resolve. She didn't listen to me this time but came back eight months later in tears because his wife was pregnant and she knew he'd never leave her now.

I told her she would meet another man, one who wasn't married, and that she needed to prepare herself for him. I took her through the Five Keys and the

Karmic Resolution Method and she finally acknowledged to me that she had a problem. "You're right, Carmen, I've created a pattern of dating married men, of dating men who will never truly be available to me, emotionally or physically." That was the first step in healing. She also saw a lot of coincidences and similarities in the way they both treated her, and even in the places they took her. Both relationships, despite being with different men, were almost the same. She knew she didn't want that type of life and set her mind to change it. When she met another married man she liked a few months later she turned him down. She knew it wouldn't be easy, but she had to hold out for what she really wanted. Soon after she did find a man who gave her the love she deserved.

Like Felicia, you have the ability to break a pattern. You can break the pattern simply with your thoughts. Behind most negative patterns is a fear or insecurity that we may not be aware of. Like Felicia, let yourself say, "I'm staying away from X. I won't let my fears and insecurities push me there." If every person you ever dated was married, or cheated on you, or was affected negatively by alcohol or drug abuse, if every person had been too possessive or controlling or jealous, you must realize these are not mere coincidences. When we repeat the same relationship patterns over and over it's because on a subconscious level we expect to be mistreated, or we don't think we deserve love. Because we're not aware of this at a conscious level, we are surprised when the same thing happens again and again.

Other distressing situations that can prevent you from moving forward with your love life may be painful breakups or divorces from the past that you have never let go of—relationships in the past that were full of negative or abusive emotions that have never been resolved, or previous relationships that never had closure.

I am often asked how long it takes to get over the pain and hurt of the past. All I can say is that it all depends on how big the hurt was, how long you have been holding on to it, and how much you have let it become accumulated karma. You can discover what's blocking you from having fulfilling relationships, eliminating negative past experiences and breaking addictive patterns with the help from the following exercise.

WIPE THE SLATE CLEAN: MEDITATION FOR ELIMINATING ADDICTIVE PATTERNS

The only way to improve your future relationships is to first free yourself from previous negative experiences or patterns. Any blocks that are holding you back usually stem from the hurts of the past and the fears and bad habits they've created.

1. Look back at the list of relationships you created from the Finding Your Dream Lover Meditation and pinpoint the relationships that upset you the most or that still have lingering negative feelings. Some of these relationships may be far in the past and some may still be fresh. Acknowledge the heartbreaks and the disappointments. Admit that this still upsets you, that it was painful and left scars, or that you wish there had been some sort of closure. We all have so many defenses built up that often, we even fool ourselves—many of us are still denying the fact that we were ever hurt. Acknowledging the hurts from past relationships is the first step toward healing and breaking a

---

pattern. As you go through this exercise stop here and be honest with yourself, let yourself feel the pain, as if for the last time. Now make a list of anyone with whom you have lingering pain or unfinished business.

2. Sit down with a pen and paper and write a letter to the person who hurt you or with whom you need closure. Perhaps you are the person who did the hurting and you need to ask for forgiveness. Write down your feelings in the most honest way you can. Write down that you know it is unhealthy for you to live with that pain or guilt. After you've admitted your pain, acknowledge the joy you shared, and remind yourself of the happy and loving times. Write that you want to replace all the pain with those moments of joy, that you prefer to remember the joy rather than the pain. You'd like to retain the happy memories and make an honest acknowledgment of the mistakes you each made, rather than hold on to anger or sadness or shame. Then forgive the person and ask them for forgiveness in return. Wish them the best in their lives and tell them it is time for you to move on.

3. Once you have written as many letters as you need to, seal each one in its own envelope, and write the name of the person on the outside of the envelope. Light a fire in the fireplace, or a candle over a sink or bathtub. Put the letters in the fire, or burn them over the sink with a candle or match. Make sure there's nothing around that could catch on fire and be careful not to burn yourself. As you watch the letters burn think of their destruction as the disintegration of any negative thoughts or patterns. Know that in burning these letters your negative feelings will dissolve. Fill your mind with thoughts of harmony, love, and forgiveness and watch the ashes and smoke as they send loving, positive energy out

into the universe. Know that you are free from
the past's negative feelings and negative patterns
from this point forward.

Learning the Lessons

One of the most important things I can show my clients
is how to stay present and be aware and resolve problems and patterns rather than walking away from them.
When I say this I'm not telling them to stay in a bad relationship; I'm telling them not to walk away from the
lessons that this relationship can teach them. Never
blame the person who came into your life and never
judge them. Everyone comes into your life for a reason,
every person is there to bring you a lesson, and every
person shows up at a certain moment for a specific
amount of time to help you gain wisdom. Often a person shows up as a messenger. You may see their appear-
ance in your life as a coincidence or as synchronicity,
but pay attention because they are there to share an important message.

In my practice I see men and women who are constantly running from their messages. Instead of looking
at what past experience can teach them about themselves, they put the blame on the other person, on their
fear of commitment, on their background and upbringing, or on the fact that they work too hard. And the
more they run and use these excuses, the less chance
they have of ever being open to love. They say they are
trying, they are dating, but they can never find the right
person. Actually the right person doesn't exist because
they haven't done the work they need to do to evolve

into a mature and loving person capable of having a relationship. But once they realize what is causing them from really not being able to find someone, once they realize the problem is within them, they can take the steps necessary to move past their excuses into a happy future.

Opening Up to Love

If our highest purpose on earth is to give and receive love, and if at our core we all *are* love, why do we resist it, why are we afraid of it, why do we push it away when we are given it, and why are we so stingy in sharing and showing our love to others? Whether you are in a romantic relationship, a friendship, or a family situation, there are many ways to form more positive, loving relationships overall.

One of the most simple ways to get love, that we so often forget, is to give love. I always tell my clients, "To get love, you must give love." You attract what you put out there. It sounds so simple and yet we all find it so difficult to do. Our egos get in the way and so we spend our time trying to protect and defend ourselves or trying to manipulate others to get what we want. This isn't loving behavior.

When clients come to me and they are not getting along with their mates I tell them, "You must allow love to bloom." A relationship is a living organism and it needs to be nurtured and fed, just like a plant, a child, a pet, or any other living creature. You can't neglect a relationship and expect it to continue to grow, or even stay alive. If you want it to flower, you must prune the weeds and give it plenty of light and water and active love. It's easy to get lazy in a relationship; it's even easier to blame your mate for your own unhappiness. But just as in your own spiritual evolution, the evolution of your relationship is something that requires awareness and dedication.

I have a list of things I tell my clients that I call the Ten Laws for a Good Marriage. These are behaviors that you can bring into your relationships that will improve them dramatically. Let go of your ego, let go of damaging emotions and watch what love can do.

Out of all of these laws, one of the hardest may be learning to forgive, because once you've forgiven it means you can't hold a grudge, you can't criticize or judge, and you can't bring up whatever it is you forgave to hurt your partner during a future argument. True forgiveness is very difficult to achieve but when it comes from a place of love and understanding—understanding that your partner is only hu-

> ### Ten Laws for a Good Marriage
> 1. Never yell at each other.
> 2. Don't be angry at the same time. If you have a conflict, let your mate talk and listen to what he or she is saying without letting your emotions take over.
> 3. Don't bring up mistakes of the past (i.e., Saying "You always," "You never," or "This is just like the time you . . .").
> 4. Don't judge and don't criticize. If you must bring a weakness to their attention, do so lovingly.
> 5. If you say or do something wrong, admit it.
> 6. Then ask for forgiveness, and mean it.
> 7. Never go to sleep with unsettled arguments (This is an oldie but a goodie).
> 8. Say something kind, loving, and complimentary to your mate every day.
> 9. Sometimes, let your mate win. Don't be so set on being "right" at the price of your relationship.
> 10. Express love every day, and allow your partner to give it by receiving it gratefully.

man, understanding that if you were in their shoes you would want forgiveness—it is one of the most healing forces in the world.

When Michael came to me he was devastated. His wife had left him for another man and had moved with this man to London, leaving Michael to raise their four-year-old son. When I told him, "She will be coming back to you," he reacted with anger. "I haven't spoken to her in over a year and I hate her for what she did to me. I don't want her in my life, even if she comes crawling back!"

"I don't blame you," I said, "but you must take her back for the sake of your child and because the relationship between you is good for both of you. She made a mistake and when she realizes it she will come back. You must forgive her and keep the karma between the two of you pure. On the conscious level you've killed your love for her, but on the subconscious level the love is still there. If you deny it it can affect your health," I warned.

"What will happen, Carmen?" he asked.

"She will separate from this other man. She is not meant to be with him. This is a test of your love and if you can practice forgiveness it will heal the pain in your soul. Don't let your ego kill your love."

Eventually his wife did come back and told Michael she had made a terrible mistake. Rather than resolving the issues in their marriage that had been wearing both of them down, she had run away. She was ready to work out their problems now and she knew that her son needed her. It wasn't easy but Michael listened to what I told him: He forgave her and took her back and now they are together raising their son. They have even opened a business together. Michael didn't allow himself to be bitter; he didn't allow himself to let his ego take over, and the lesson he learned about his own capacity for love has made him a different person.

Some of you reading this may think it was wrong for Michael to take her back; you may think I gave him bad advice and that such unfaithfulness is unforgivable. But where is the wisdom in that? Wisdom comes from letting go of anger, revenge, bitterness, cynicism, and choosing to celebrate love. All of us make mistakes; nobody is perfect, as the Latin proverb says *Errare Humanum Est*, to err is human. Mistakes are part of the human system. The key is not to let them ruin you but rather to treat them as opportunities to learn.

Relationships are one of the best ways for us to evolve spiritually because it is in loving other people that our egos and emotions have the greatest opportunity to run amok. This is true of romantic relationships, friendships, the way we relate to our family, and the way we relate to coworkers, our neighbors, and strangers on the street. We all come from a place of divine love and it is our mission to live in that place of love here on earth. When we don't, it can have profound effects on our health—both our physical and emotional well-being—as you'll see in the next chapter.

CHAPTER SIX

Healing Karmic Wounds

When I see someone for the first time, I know right away if they have a problem with the physical body. I always discuss health issues in my readings. If you have a thyroid problem, a heart problem, a liver problem, too much sugar or not enough minerals in the diet, pain, visual, dental, or back problems, I recognize it right away. And I always tell my clients because if they are aware of it, they can do something to catch it before it's too late. Many health problems start small and escalate so the sooner there is an awareness of the problem, the sooner healing can begin.

I can also recognize past health problems in people. A famous Hollywood entertainment lawyer once came to see me, wearing a suit and a tie. He had heard about me from one of his own clients and wasn't sure why he was coming to see me but was curious because of what he'd heard. He was astounded when the first thing I said to him was, "There's a problem with your chest; what is it?" He took off his tie and jacket, opened his shirt and showed me a huge scar; he had just had open-heart surgery a few weeks before. Although he was doing fine physically, until he came to see me he couldn't admit what a frightening and life-changing event this surgery had been for him. He came to realize how short life can be and also how the choices he made every day affected his health.

The doorman at my office building was always skeptical about what I did until I walked in one day and said to him, "You were robbed and stabbed recently, weren't you?" He was shocked. He, too, showed me his scar and said he hadn't told anybody else about it. Keeping his pain a secret was a burden for him and he was having a tough time recovering emotionally from the attack. Having me acknowledge his pain also helped him in the healing process. And he never doubted my abilities again!

Recognizing people's physical problems and health issues is actually how I started doing the work I do as a metaphysical intuitive. When I first got married and moved to the United States I stopped my singing career, except for singing in Virgil's restaurant once in a while, and I went to work for my uncle, who is a well-known oncologist. One day a patient came in, a woman in her fifties, and as soon as I saw her all of these images came into my mind, and I couldn't help myself, I had to tell her about them. I said, "There's a person in the distance, somewhere in the Middle East, who is going to call you and tell you there's been a problem. Someone whose name starts with *G* is going to have a heart attack. You're going to get a phone message in three hours." She didn't know what to think of me. I think she was stunned that I would say this to her, especially since I didn't know her. The next day she called me and said that her husband, George, was in Saudi Arabia on business and had had a heart attack. She was upset, but because she had a warning she felt better prepared to handle the situation. She told me, "Carmen, I don't know how you knew this but you have to do this work. You can use this to help people." She began sending her friends to me and eventually, I became so busy I had to leave my uncle's office to do this work full-time.

Over the years I've found that as much as life is expressed in the body through karmic experiences, the way the body looks, the form of the body, the weaknesses and illnesses of the body are also karmic expressions.

Although I'm not a medical doctor and would never presume to heal a client without the aid of the medical system, I do see myself as a healer. I help in the healing process in two ways. The first is my ability to identify the problem and help you recognize it; healing can only begin when the problem is acknowledged. The second is my ability to transfer positive healing energy.

The Mudava Phenomenon

I was first introduced to the basic principles of healing as a child. At that time in Romania everyone was talking about a man called Constantin Mudava and the so-called, "Mudava Phenomenon." Mudava was a middle-aged man who claimed to have the gift of healing through his hands. He said he had inherited the gift from his grandfather who had been able to heal himself from sickness and disease with his left hand and, as a result, lived to be 118 years old! He would raise his left hand and whatever diseases he had would disappear.

Although people were skeptical at first, the Mudava Phenomenon spread through Romania and people from all over were coming to him to be healed. Mudava was a highly respected man and scientist who had graduated from the University of Physics and had put himself through all kinds of tests to prove his gift and more important, to try to understand the source of his healing powers. He took electrographs and photos to show the changes in people's bodies after he performed the transfer of energy to them. Although he never pinpointed how this energy healing worked from a scientific standpoint, his belief was that we shouldn't be afraid of what we don't understand.

My only experience with Mudava was through a woman in my neighborhood who went to see him. Her experience profoundly affected my desire to learn more about this field. This was in 1970 and she had breast cancer. The tumor was quite large. This was long before the time of breast cancer awareness and Romania did not have the best medical system, so this woman's chances for survival were slim. She saw Mudava twice and after the second time her tumor opened up and a lot of infected substances came out. Once the sore closed up a few weeks later, she was completely healed.

The Mudava Phenomenon was explained through a theory that came to be known as bioenergy. As I've said before, everything is made of energy: a table, a glass, a plant, an animal, a person. All of the molecules of the human body are surrounded by small electromagnetic fields and all of these fields combine to create one large "biofield" surrounding the individual. This energy, or biofield, has a frequency and each object and each individual operates at a different frequency. People with a higher frequency, a higher state of vibration, also have a higher state of perception. The level of a person's vibrational energy is what makes them unique.

A healer like Mudava has a biofield that works at a higher level of perception, that takes divine energy from the Invisible World and uses its healing power. A person with a pure and balanced biofield can identify imbalance in another person's biofield and then transfer energy to him. This isn't done through scientific or intellectual knowledge, it is done through a deep spiritual understanding and practice.

Our biofield is profoundly affected by the energy we take in and put out, whether positive or negative. There is also a close relationship between the level of positivity or negativity in our biofield and our mental, emotional, and physical states. If there is a higher level of positive energy—meaning energy that comes from the Invisible World—then our mental, emotional, and physical states will be more positive. Negative energy in our field throws us off balance and creates illness and emotional disturbances. This means the spiritual, invisible energies that come in the form of memory or karma, have a powerful effect over our health and our ability to maintain our health. When we resolve our karma, we clear our biofield by eliminating negative blocks and allowing healing, positive energy to flow through us, bringing us back to health and wholeness.

We all have a biofield, and even though it's invisible, like the air we breathe, it is just as crucial to our well-being. Commonly called an aura, it is like an envelope protecting us, an envelope of light that is a reflection of the energy we are absorbing and sending out. The aura should be light and bright and if it is, it means all is well. If not, something is going wrong.

Just because the idea of a biofield doesn't exist in medical studies and research doesn't mean it doesn't exist and yield results. In 1992 the National Institutes of Health published a report called "Alternative Medicine: Expanding Medical Horizons" that defined the phenomenon of the biofield. I think it's important that we continue to explore this area and do research so that we can come to know how it works—I think it's the future of medicine. The less closed-minded we are, the more open we are to infinite possibilities, and the more likely we are to gain understanding and be able to use this understanding to help ourselves.

Twenty-seven years after Mudava, researchers are beginning to agree that living organisms are surrounded by an energetic aura. And the idea of energy healing is becoming more and more common. The concept of healing by touch is something that has been practiced for hundreds, even thousands of years, most notably in traditional Chinese medicine with practices like acupuncture. There are many types of energeticists and many different methods to do this but the same principles behind energy healing are what drive people toward practices like Qi Gong, yoga, meditation, Reiki, deep breathing, and tai chi, which are all ways of creating and maintaining balance in your own energetic system.

The way that energy translates into matter, the way it gets into our body, is through our major energy points, called chakras. There are seven chakras or energy points that correspond with the nerves located along the spine. Each chakra influences and regulates certain organs and characteristics and if a particular chakra is blocked from receiving energy or is receiving negative energy, those organs and aspects of a person will be affected. I will discuss the chakras in more detail and show you how to tune in to them later in this chapter.

Every cell and organ in the body, then, is like a sponge that absorbs and accumulates bioenergy. Every human being, as an accumulator of energy, is connected to the higher cosmic system of energy, meaning we are affected profoundly by the energy that is all around us, whether we realize it or not. To put this in the simplest terms possible, if we absorb negative energy we get sick; if we absorb positive energy we remain healthy. Healers are able to draw on positive cosmic energy and transfer it into themselves or another person. The person absorbs the positive energy and goes back into balance.

When I talk about cosmic energy I mean the energy from the Invisible World, the infinite universe. This cosmic energy, what I call the Universal Healing Energy, is what we return to, and what we are made of, outside of our physical body. In other words, when we die, we shed our body but our energy remains and we reunite with the cosmic energy. This energy can not only help cure disease on the physical level but can also help on a mental and emotional level. A lot of what I do in my own work is to transfer this energy into the people who come to me. They may come to me confused or depressed, angry or discouraged, but during my sessions I give them pure cosmic energy and they leave with hope in their hearts. They feel better and ready to start a new life and a new way of thinking.

Although we live in the physical world of time, space, and matter, we all need to absorb cosmic energy in order to be alive. The more we take, the better we feel, and the longer we live. Meditation and prayer are so important because they are such an effective way of absorbing that Universal Healing Energy. When the energy stops going through us physically then our bodies die. If the energy isn't flowing freely within us physically, we get sick. The word disease means disintegrate or disorder. When the energy and the physical body disintegrate, life stops. When energy isn't flowing freely through a certain part of our body, we get cancer or other illnesses.

Recognizing and Acknowledging Health Problems

In my work I can see the aura of people's biofields, which is how I can point out the sick parts of their body, and know the surgeries or problems in the past they may have had. I can feel the level of their blood pressure, their cholesterol and whether or not certain things are missing from the body.

For example, when Isabelle came to me and sat down, I was aware immediately that she was totally imbalanced physically. She was missing a lot of minerals in her blood. I told her this and she said, "No, you don't understand, I'm not coming to you with a physical problem. I'm here because I suffer from terrible anxiety; I've been having panic attacks and feel extremely weak." I told her it was because her levels of calcium, iron, and magnesium were too low. Several weeks later she called me and said she had gone to a new doctor who did some blood tests and diagnosed her with tetany, a disease that stems from the body not absorbing calcium that manifests in muscle contractions that could be interpreted as panic attacks. Usually, when operating at a high level of awareness, you can recognize problems without any type of medical test.

When it comes to health, "prediction for prevention" is particularly important. Recognizing and acknowledging a health problem has obvious benefits for the sooner you acknowledge it, the sooner you can get treatment. Like karma, physical problems can accumulate over time and become that much more difficult to reverse or cure. Despite this, you'd be amazed how many people actively deny that anything is wrong and are afraid to go to the doctor.

A mother and daughter came to me because the mother was worried about the daughter's smoking. She wanted to know if the smoking had permanently damaged her daughter's health, hoping I might scare her into quitting. I saw immediately that the mother herself had a problem with her heart from years of smoking— although she had quit nearly a decade before—and warned her about it. She saw her doctor and was able to go on heart medication before the problem became life-threatening. The mother was worried about how smoking was affecting her daughter's health and yet she was ignoring how it had damaged her own! I think that subconsciously, the mother knew something was wrong with her heart but was afraid to face it. She came to see me partly out of genuine concern for her daughter's health but also to acknowledge and confirm her suspicions about her own.

Another case in point is Susan, who had a broken arm when she came to me for a reading. She couldn't work until her arm healed and she was worried that it was taking too long. When I sense a medical emergency, I move quickly. I told her, "Never mind your arm, your arm will be fine, but you have a much bigger problem, which is a tumor in your uterus." She gasped in horror, and immediately went to her doctor, who did find a tumor. She was on the operating table within a week to get it removed. She later told me I saved her life, but the real work started when she came back for additional readings and was able to get in touch with the "stuck" energy that had been lodged in her womb for decades.

Once you bring a problem to the surface, and face it, healing can begin. I also think that healing takes place when a person begins to put order in his life, when he restores balance. One of the most effective ways to restore balance and maintain a sense of wholeness is by resolving your karma in your daily life. You will find that resolving your karma will make you feel better and prevent many types of illnesses and physical complaints. Resolving your karma strengthens your immune system! When people get enmeshed in emotional drama, their energy field becomes vulnerable and that's when they can get sick. Disease is dis-ease, disassociating from the whole. We aren't meant to be divided. I can show you how to be in tune with your own health. Once you realize that we are all made of energy, you can acknowledge that we get sick at the energetic level first and then on the physical level. So often there are things in our past that we haven't accepted and until we acknowledge our own actions and thought patterns, we can't begin to heal. Every affliction in the mind will influence the function of the body.

A Psychic Checkup

I have created a system I call a Psychic Checkup, which is a bioenergetic method of healing by creating body awareness and listening to your body's messages, focusing on each of the seven chakras. By meditating on the different energy points that correlate to different parts of the body you create physical and emotional awareness, begin to listen to what your body is telling you, and become aware of any bad karma you are holding onto. In this way health problems can be identified before they get out of control. I've found that this practice can be a meaningful preventative and diagnostic tool and it can create tremendous healing by bringing positive energy into each of your major energy points.

This exercise is not meant to heal sickness but to identify the causes of illness, prevent illness through acknowledging and recognizing symptoms, and to lessen pain and symptoms. In this exercise you will connect your mind and awareness to your physical life where the problems of the ego and emotions go. Oftentimes illness is caused by carrying deep within us unresolved stress, tension, or feelings of anger, hurt, hostility, loneliness, hopelessness, and sadness. So many illnesses are related to repressed feelings and chronic stress that get stuck at an energy point and begin to wreak havoc on the correlating part of our body.

Stress is the number one killer in our world; it is at the source of most diseases and it can paralyze you. Some people receive stress in their bodies and others in their minds. In order to do this exercise you must eliminate stress by reaching a deep state of relaxation. Stress prevents us from concentrating and prevents us from connecting and developing awareness. In order to relax and concentrate, begin by putting all of your focus on your breath; breathe intensely and watch your breath instead of the world outside of you. Forget about your computer, this book, the walls around you, or any noise. Keep breathing and shift your attention from the outer world to your inner world, your own sanctuary of feelings, emotions, and physical sensations.

I am going to take you through the seven energy points of the body, to take your attention through every part of your entire body from your toes up to your head, and as you go through, listen to what your body has to say. Notice any tension, any sensations, any feelings you have lodged anywhere in the physical. The body has tremendous intelligence and can heal itself. Be aware if anyone or anything is the cause of your stress or negative emotions out in the world. When you become aware of something you can say it out loud, or write it down; talk about what is making you miserable or frustrated, or any of the feelings you have. Then focus on that part of the body, the chakra where the feeling came up, and imagine the chakra being open, with positive energy flowing through it, and replace any negative feelings with a feeling of happiness.

First Chakra: The Root Chakra/ Self-Preservation

The root chakra is associated with the earth and is located at the base of the spine. It is oriented to self-preservation and represents stability, being grounded in the physical being, physical health, survival, and prosperity. It controls the digestive system, especially the intestines, and the kidneys. If it is blocked in any way you will experience insecurity and lack of confidence, anxiety, constipation, problems with your teeth, problems with your spine (back problems and injuries), joint and bone problems.

Second Chakra: Navel Chakra/ Self-Gratification

This chakra regulates the genitals and sexual energy and is located in the abdomen, genitals, and lower back. It is oriented toward self-gratification and brings a feeling of fluidity and adaptability, pleasure and sensation, and a connection to others through our emotions. When energy is stuck here we have nervousness, gall bladder infections, liver problems, migraines, lower back pain, sexual dysfunction, depression, low energy and apathy, lethargy, and problems with the nervous system.

Third Chakra: Solar Plexus/Self-Definition

This chakra is the seat of the personality, the ego, and is located in the solar plexus. It is oriented toward self-definition. It is your center of power, purpose, vitality, and self-esteem. It is also where you assimilate food. If it isn't open enough you will experience sadness, egotism, repressed emotions, muscular tension, poor metabolism, and stomach problems.

Fourth Chakra: The Heart Chakra/ Self-Acceptance

This is located in your heart area, in the vertebrae opposite the main artery that brings blood to your heart. It is oriented toward self-acceptance and it is where you find peace and balance, compassion, and it allows you to love deeply and have satisfying relationships. If it is blocked you will have lung problems, breathing problems, skin problems, difficulties in receiving love, negative thinking, and a closed heart.

Fifth Chakra: The Throat Chakra/ Self-Expression

This chakra is located at the base of the neck, behind your throat and is the center of your vocal expression and personal integrity. It is oriented toward self-expression and rules your creativity and ability to communicate. If it is blocked you will experience communication problems, feel overwhelmed, deny responsibility, have weight problems, and frequent colds and infections.

Sixth Chakra: The Third Eye/Self-Reflection

This chakra is located at the brow, between your two eyes, near the pituitary gland. It is oriented toward self-reflection and when it is open you are able to merge consciousness with the subconscious. It is your center of intuition and imagination. Through this chakra you are able to go beyond earthly goals. If it is blocked you will experience eye and vision problems, problems with concentration, and you will be critical and judgmental.

Seventh Chakra: Crown of the Head/ Self-Knowledge

This chakra is located at the top of your head, near the cerebral cortex and is your center of awareness. It is the main connection between the Visible World and the Invisible World. It is oriented toward self-knowledge and helps bring about wisdom, understanding, and spiritual connection. If this chakra is blocked you will experience a lack of confidence, problems with the adrenal glands, thyroid, and parathyroid.

After you've scanned the body, developed awareness of areas where you are blocked, continue to breathe deeply and through a prayer ask for the negative emotions to be released. Imagine a brilliant white light surrounding each particular chakra, starting at the first chakra and moving up the body to the crown of your head. At each chakra ask for wholeness and continued awareness. If you do this once a month, you should be able to stay on top of potential health problems.

The Danger of Negativity

I've always said that we die a little with each negative thought. In our biofield any wrong information will manifest in something physical. There is a strong correlation between our karma and our health and mental and physical well-being. Every negative thought will strike the body somewhere.

When Marjorie came to me she was very sad about her husband. They had been married for five years and they were both disappointed in the marriage and had tried to go to counseling to resolve their problems to no avail. Recently, she had found out that both her husband and her best friend were betraying her by having an affair, and that led her to incredible despair. She felt unloved and unsupported. She had been trying so hard to make the relationship work and was in the middle of a terrible emotional crisis. She felt she had proved to be unlovable and she couldn't see it changing in the future. I warned her not to be so hard on herself, to take it easy and do nurturing things for herself to try to heal. She was in so much pain and felt so hopeless I knew it would manifest itself somehow in her health.

Half a year later she was diagnosed with breast cancer. Her immune system was vulnerable because her biofield had so much negativity. This is not to say she brought sickness upon herself—that's not what I'm saying at all. No one can be blamed for getting sick. What I am saying is that when we are surrounded by negativity our strength weakens, our body becomes vulnerable and prey to illness. Every negative thought has a physiological correlation. The only way to remain physically strong is to try not to allow our field to become vulnerable. The more positive the field, the easier it is for our bodies to fight off the negative that will manifest in the physical. Over the years I have seen many cases of breast and uterine cancer in women after their husbands have betrayed them. My work has always been to make them aware of the danger involved in holding on to anger. They always ask me, "But Carmen, where is God? First my husband betrays me and now I have cancer." I tell them God is pure forgiveness. If you forgive, you will help yourself.

Negativity is contagious, and so is positivity. It can affect us individually and it can affect large groups of people. Look at the bad karma and negativity of Hitler that poisoned millions. His negativity spread throughout the world and his karma became the world's group karma that we all have to heal.

I'll never forget when I was in college, writing my thesis in order to graduate. I had chosen Camus, a French writer, who was the father of existentialism. I think existentialism appealed to me because it stressed the individual's freedom to make his own life choices and to accept responsibility for the consequences of his actions. What I didn't fully grasp, until I delved further into it, was that existentialism also assumes that we all live as isolated individuals in a hostile or indifferent universe. There is no belief in a divine order or cosmic energy.

As I started to study Camus's notebooks to understand his philosophical thinking, I became incredibly depressed. He felt that everything is useless, everything we try to build will be destroyed, and all we get in the end is to be put in the grave. I almost had a nervous breakdown! I did get incredibly sick. I was so demoralized I eventually changed the subject of my thesis. I was young then, only twenty-one, and my life experience was in some ways still limited, but I knew, from my own experiences with the Invisible World and the words from my grandfather, that Camus was terribly wrong. And yet he and the existentialist movement had tremendous influence over the thinking of the twentieth century. And much of the terrible events in the world in the twentieth century seemed to reflect this. But what good comes from thinking in such a way? Why would anyone choose this type of belief system? It is beyond me as it will only lead to further despair and prevent us, as individuals and as a species, from evolving.

Ever since that experience I have spent the past twenty years reflecting on how we all develop our own belief systems and how they affect the outcome of our lives. Yes, we all live here on earth for a short time, some shorter than others, and some of us die tragically. There are certain things in our fate that we cannot change. We will all suffer, have our problems, and develop illness and physical limitations from time to time. I'm not immune to pain and suffering—none of us are. In spite of the things we can't change, we *can* change our way of thinking. We can choose to make our lives as enjoyable as possible, despite setbacks and suffering, or we can add to our own suffering. We can heal; we can make our lives richer; it is within our reach.

If you want to be healthy, you have to give up negative feelings whether they involve your family, your friends, your love life, or your destiny. Love and forgiveness and faith all have a powerful role for us and our state of health. Our love for other people is crucial for healing and spiritual growth. Any time in life that we kill love, we can expect something catastrophic to happen because we have destroyed our unity with God. Love is the most powerful way to demonstrate our unity with the divine energy of the universe and love is incredibly powerful—it is more powerful than any negativity and will always be a healing force. I always found it interesting that the word religion has its roots in the Latin word "religare," which means to bind or tie, a union. The origin of religion was to be one with God. The word yoga means the same thing, unity. If you are a believer, whether through religion or yoga or your own combination of spiritual philosophy, you are absorbing more of God's loving energy into your biofield.

One of the areas where we can absorb negativity the most is in our families. The bonds of family are close and energy transfers and flows freely between family members, often on a subconscious level. Here, more than anywhere, it is important to show love and forgiveness and to recognize when you must address and heal your own family karma. The bond between mother and daughter is one of the closest bonds, as I saw only too well in a strange case where the mother's karma was passed on to the daughter.

When Jill was twenty years old she was involved in a relationship with a man and found out that the man was also involved with somebody else. She was young, shocked, and devastated, and vowed she would never let another man hurt her again. After breaking off with him, she discovered that she was pregnant and she had a daughter, Ann. Never telling the father, she raised Ann on her own. Ann is now thirty-eight and Jill is fifty-nine and throughout their life together Jill has never even gone on a date with another man and Ann has never had a relationship that lasted longer than two months. Jill's negative attitudes toward men have been passed on to her daughter. The two of them live together and they are both unhappy; they both suffer from heavy karma and have suffered a variety of health problems. Each one's negativity feeds off the other's and neither one understands where God is in their lives. And Ann can't understand why she never found a relationship that lasted!

I explained to Jill, "Your lifelong anger at Ann's father and the way you killed your love for him and for all men has been transferred to your daughter. Even though she says she wants a relationship, her subconscious won't allow it." I've tried to move Jill to a place of healthier mental and emotional energy, but she doesn't want to understand and her life approach is very existential in its nature. She doesn't trust anyone and she doesn't believe in God. All because of something that happened almost forty years ago!

It's a very unhappy situation and since I couldn't get through to Jill, I tried to talk to her daughter. I told Ann that it was time for her to move out on her own and try to build a life for herself, free from her mother, while still loving her mother. The bond is too strong and too unhealthy. Ann would not leave her mother, but she did recently meet a man who said that he loved her and wanted to move in with her, but not with her mother. He is trying to make her choose.

I have prayed that Ann will choose happiness with this man, to continue to love her mother but to allow herself to have a better life. At this point, I don't know what she will do but I can tell you that if she doesn't leave she will be bitter. The heavy karma between her and her mother will never be lifted, and her health problems will only get worse. I want her to see that her family karma, the belief system she has as a result, and her health are all interconnected. She must analyze why she holds on to the belief system she does, resolve it, and try to move on. If Jill and Ann could learn to forgive and approach each other with love, they would both be happier and healthier.

Using Your Own Healing Energy

When I was twenty-eight my father was diagnosed with thyroid cancer and the doctor told him he had three months to live. I went to the doctor with my father and I said, "No, he's not going to die; he's going to live for another eight years." As you can imagine, the doctor didn't pay much attention to me and figured I was in denial. My father was scheduled to go into surgery, but it was winter and the night before the surgery he fell on the ice and broke his knee and had to postpone the surgery until his knee had healed. The doctor was extremely concerned because he was afraid the cancer would spread and become inoperable.

My father was in a cast for six months and clearly had outlived his three-month diagnosis. When the cast was taken off he was given another round of tests and the cancer was completely gone. He lived for eight more years and eventually died of a stroke.

In the case of my father, I used my own healing energy by praying for him to get better. And I prayed often and fervently! Prayers are extremely powerful energy and when we pray we absorb the energy of the universe and direct it outward. Our own energy and that of the people we pray for get stronger. One of my favorite authors is Larry Dossey, M.D., who reveals in his research, in his book *Prayer Is Good Medicine,* that this is scientifically true. Prayers empower the energetic system. They are a way to create peace within yourself and to protect negative energy from external forces from getting into your biofield.

I will always remember the way my own mother used to pray. She would read the Bible with her hands facing up to the sky, speaking out loud and even crying. She created a dialogue with God, let him know her problems and her greatest desires and wishes. She asked him for forgiveness for her wrongdoing, and she prayed for the well-being of others in her life. She used to tell me, "Carmen, you've made me a believer in the Invisible World and you've helped me connect with God in a much stronger way." I bought her a book of psalms and for the last seven years of her life she read it every day. Her prayers helped her purify her biofield and prepared her for leaving the physical body and reuniting with God.

We gather a lot of impurities into our biofield every day from our environment and our daily thoughts and actions. As we already know, every action creates a good or bad result, a reflection on your body or your mind. If you look in a mirror and smile, the face in the mirror will smile back. It all depends on whether you want to smile. The way to eliminate wrong action, wrong thoughts, and wrong habits is through prayers. Prayers are the way to correct all that you said or did wrong over the course of the day. Prayers are a powerful way to resolve karma.

Use your voice to talk to God. The Buddhists used to say, "The mouth is the front-gate of all misfortune." It means, think twice before you speak. Words are very powerful. The negative words you say, whether out loud to others or in negative self-talk to yourself, have a powerful impact. Positive words are just as powerful, but too often we forget to be positive during the stress of our day. At night, before you go to sleep, you can use your voice to talk to God, to reconnect with the divine energy of the universe. Your prayers are the voice of divinity within you. Prayers are the light of knowledge. Prayer is a state of peace, ecstasy, and devotion. When you pray you are speaking from your truest self. Prayers are the way to repair disconnection, to feel whole again. Prayers heal your field of energy; they purify the karmic thoughts and actions. Prayers will create balance. And prayers can heal.

Prayers are a powerful way to align your own karma with the divine. It is using all of your efforts to live your life without ego in order to purify your spirit as an instrument through which to reach divinity. To help you create your own healing energy I have come up with the following exercise.

TAPPING THE UNIVERSAL LIFE FORCE

You can pray anywhere, anytime, but the most powerful way to pray is in your own room, far from any outside influences, and to pray sincerely using your own words, telling God your hopes and dreams, as well as your pains. Create a special, sacred place in which to talk to God and pray regularly, sincerely, and humbly.

A person is made up of what he or she believes. The way you believe is the way you will be. You are what you pray for. The divine rarely expresses itself directly upon

the lives of people on earth. The sequences and the trans-
formations in us are to be noticed at the level of signs
and symbols.

• Pray to see the signs in your life in order to gain
  wisdom.

• Pray for wisdom to see the light from above.

• Pray for greater knowledge and self-awareness.

• Pray in gratitude for the miracle that is your life.

• Pray for protection from negativity from outside forces
  and from the negativity of your own mind.

• Pray for your own health and well-being.

• Pray for the health and well-being of your family and
  loved ones.

• Pray for serenity.

• Pray for abundance.

• Pray for the well-being of your friends and be thankful
  for their friendship and generosity.

• Pray for spiritual evolution.

• Pray for those in need.

• Pray for those who are dead.

• Pray to be able to hear God and heed the wisdom.

• Pray to be a better person.

• Pray for forgiveness for any wrongdoing or harsh words
  that day.

• Pray for peace in the world; pray for a better world.

You can pray in this simple way when you wake up in
the morning, before you go to sleep, before eating, before
an important event. Prayer is not just for the religious,

and you do not have to pray in any specific way or to any specific god or memorize specific prayers to gain the benefits.

Prayer is about connecting to the divine, recognizing and clearing the karmic events of the day, and speaking out your pains and desires from the place of your true self. Praying daily will protect you from negativity, will make you more in control of events and decisions, and will give you a much healthier body and mind. Practice this exercise on a daily basis and see the miracles that begin to take place in your life. These miracles will be big and small. Don't have doubt, pray and believe and you will find you feel much more at peace, less stressed, and your heart will fill with hope and gratitude and a stronger sense of well-being.

The thought process has a profound effect on your health and well-being, so negative and positive thoughts will have negative and positive results. One of the best ways to be in a consistent state of positive thought is to align yourself to your karmic life purpose, which I'll explain in the next chapter.

CHAPTER SEVEN

Discovering Your Karmic Life Purpose

Often the reason people come to me, and why they go to any type of intuitive or psychic, is to have someone "tell them their future." They are so bored or unhappy or stuck where they are in their lives that they are desperate for someone to tell them that there's hope, that things will change, that there is the potential for happiness. And of course, there *is* hope, things *can* change and your potential for happiness *can* be realized. But when they come to me to find out their future, what they are really asking is, "What is my purpose?" They find themselves going through the daily grind and they aren't feeling inspired. They've lost touch with their divine nature because they haven't yet realized their life's purpose. And if you don't know what it is you're on earth to do, you aren't doing it and there's going to be this constant gnawing dissatisfaction. Even more important, fulfilling your life's purpose plays an essential role in helping to resolve your karma.

Our purpose for living is bigger than we are and too often we are afraid to go against convention or the confines of our upbringing to seek out our true selves, our gifts, our talents, and our abilities to express ourselves. We are all here to use our God-given gifts and abilities to help one another, to serve one another and, if possible, to help humanity as a whole. For some people their purpose is very clear to them because they have heard a calling: monks, priests, nuns, rabbis may hear a calling to serve God, and artists, writers, musicians whose talents come to them at an early age, also have their own calling and a clear message they want to express. Someone like Mozart, who was playing accomplished music at age five doesn't need to work out his life's purpose— it was clear from the minute he was born and was the continuation of his karma from a past life. For the rest of us it isn't as easy to know our purpose but it is our responsibility to find it. The fast pace and endless distractions of life today can make it difficult for us to hear and heed our true purpose, but life without purpose is meaningless.

Several years ago Bob came to see me. He was an extremely successful trader on the stock exchange and had a demanding and stressful job that left him little time for other pursuits. He made a lot of money for his clients and for himself and he felt that was good enough. He had been raised to believe that as a man a large part of his worth was based on how much money he could make, how well he could provide for a family, and he didn't "waste his time" pondering questions like, "What is my purpose?" I kept telling him not to place all his self-worth on how much money he made. I encouraged him to spend more time focusing on creating a family and building relationships that would serve as a support system. And I told him to develop other interests and to invest in developing a spiritual life.

He had been flying high and reinvesting all of his own money into the market but saw that things were in a serious downturn and came to me to find out what I thought would happen. This was many years ago and at this point I had already predicted the stock market crash of 1987 on television. I had warned him to be prepared, and to put money aside, but he never listened. When it actually happened, he was desperate. I felt sorry for him because he was so miserable and yet he had allowed his self-worth and life purpose to revolve around an illusion—the state of something as volatile and unreliable as the stock market. When things took a downturn he felt completely lost and had no reservoirs of true self-worth to rely on. You hear about people jumping out of windows in 1929 when the stock market crashed—even in 1987 some people did—and you have to ask yourself, didn't these people think the value of their lives was worth more than that? Yes, losing a lot of money is an unhappy situation and can create painful disruptions in your lifestyle, but it shouldn't make you feel your life is worthless. Had he listened to my advice, he would have been better prepared, but he was only interested in his monetary investments, not his spiritual or emotional investments.

I see so many people like this, who have no real satisfaction, who act like robots, making money to survive, to buy nice things, to gratify their egos, and yet they're not happy. How ironic that when these symbols of achievement are taken from them, they feel devastated—they have no idea how to fill the emptiness. They are suffering from a crisis in meaning because they have lost their value system or had a faulty one to begin with.

A Crisis of Values

When I was growing up in Romania, my father had a good job working at the local bank and we had what we needed. We were satisfied. We weren't rich and we weren't poor and money really wasn't an issue for us. We had our family and friends around us. We supported and loved one another; my parents worked hard but they didn't live to work. They had their priorities in order and didn't let earning a living take place over everything else in their lives. It would have been ludicrous then to even imagine the word "workaholic." People would have thought you were crazy! When Ceausescu came into power, life became a lot more difficult for us. Food and many basic things we took for granted were harder to come by, and even worse was this stifling sense of feeling controlled, boxed in. I remember my father waking up at 2 A.M. to wait in line for hours for just two bottles of milk with detergent in them. But somehow we still knew what we valued and loved, and we still found ways to get by and be happy.

In today's world we are so business-oriented and money-focused, that often, we lose sight of our higher purpose, living our lives with a vague sense of dissatisfaction as a result. Our value system as a society and as individuals is confused and we are seeing and feeling the negative consequences. Living in a consumer culture certainly has its benefits and we have a much higher standard of living than our parents and grandparents, and yet something has been lost when we don't have time to be with our families and loved ones. Why do we all work so much? Why do we let work take priority over our friends and family? When everyone is working so much, no one has time to love and support one another. And we try to make up for that lack of support by overeating and overbuying and developing all types of soul-murdering addictions. Who could have dreamed of eating disorders fifty years ago? When drugs are killing our children, when our children are killing other children, we know something is terribly wrong. We've lost our connection to other people and most important, we've lost our connection to our true selves, to our essence. I think it's crucial that people move beyond physical desires and physical satisfaction and immediate gratification of all of our needs, if we are ever to find fulfillment in life and move forward as individuals and as a society.

So how do we do that? How do we stop the treadmill that the whole world seems to be on? Sometimes it feels that you either keep up the pace or get knocked off. Life has become expensive and if we're going to have a roof over our heads, and our children educated, we need to work hard to keep up. The problem with this is that it will never make us happy, and ultimately, it is meaningless. Yes, we all want to survive, but do we really need to have the best of everything? Is that really going to make us happy? Is it going to reduce our stress levels? Is it going to help us give and receive love? Is it going to help us gain wisdom? I don't think so. It's time to rethink our values and look at the price we are paying for what we have come to think of as success.

The Karma of Money

One of the biggest areas where we lose sight of our values is money. What is money anyway? Money is nothing more than something we use to get other things that we want. To me, money is energy and it has its own karma. Money energy, like karma, needs to be kept in balance or it will haunt and control you.

Too much money will throw you off balance; it can make you selfish, egotistical, mean, and addicted. And worst of all, it keeps you attached to the ground, to the earth energy. You've probably heard the saying, "You can't take it with you." Well, you can't. When you leave the earth you aren't taking anything with you except your soul and your karma. Not your bank account, or china and crystal, or jewelry or clothes. Not your house and all the furniture and belongings in it, and not your car. On the other side you have only your soul, so it is far more important to accumulate wisdom in your soul than it is to accumulate possessions, which only give more power to the ego and diminish the soul's ability to evolve.

On the other hand, having too little money also creates problems. God wants everyone to have enough. When people live in poverty it creates tremendous problems, disease, corruption, and suffering. People who don't have their basic needs met, who don't have food or a roof over their heads, who must struggle day after day, are also tied to the earth energy. Their lack creates an imbalance and doesn't allow them to think about the nature of their souls. It can create such need that they are willing to do anything just to have their basic needs met and this can lead to theft, murder, hatred, and jealousy. Look at Afghanistan for example. This is a country with so much poverty that the people felt powerless enough to allow the Taliban to take over and repress them even further. That same poverty and repression breeds hatred for people who have what they don't. This creates a breeding ground for terrorists, and leads to war. In Afghanistan there is also a huge drug trade. Farmers there grow poppies that are made into heroin, because it's the only lucrative crop the country has. People without money grow and sell drugs to people with money who take drugs to forget how empty they feel. What a crazy situation!

Whenever life revolves around money you are bound to feel empty. The more you run for money, the farther away you get from your true self, the less sense life makes, and the less you will eventually have. Thinking that money is your life supply, your security, your survival, and your support is disconnecting and devaluing your essence. It's ignoring the divine in you and it prevents you from having faith in yourself. Every person is meant to have enough. It is natural for you to have what you need, but if you block the natural field of financial energy from manifesting around you, you will feel more worried and more trapped.

Many people come to me and say, "Carmen, why don't I have the money I need? I'm working so hard." First, what you think you need may be different from what you really need. Second, money, as energy, has to flow to manifest and if you're afraid or blocked for some reason, if you have some past karma involving money that hasn't been resolved, the energy will not manifest. Money is just an effect; the cause is your mind. If you allow the effect, in this case money, to take control and undermine the cause, you will be victimized by it. If you think of your mind as the cause, money will flow. This means not being afraid of having money, being responsible with it, earning and using it in an honorable way that stems from who you truly are, and never, ever mistaking it for your life's purpose.

I see so many people who have everything in the world but they can't find happiness in their private lives. Because they have the wrong ideas, they aren't operating from the place of self-knowledge or self-trust from their soul. They say, "I'm never going to find someone who loves me just for me; they love the money" or "I just don't want to be with anyone unless they have as much money as I do" or even, "I can only marry someone who makes more money than I do." With beliefs like that they won't be able to find happiness even with all the money in the world because they are going into what they call "love" with ideas that have nothing to do with love!

These people have been warped by their rich parents, or their egos, or the poor values of society. They feel lost, hopeless, and misunderstood. There are breakups in their families, alcoholism, divorce, ill-will, and hatred. They start to anticipate bad things happening to them and so bad things do happen. Money doesn't bring them anything in the end.

The real purpose of existence is the growth of the spirit. How can you grow with the wrong ideas in your mind? If you are all about accumulation and don't care that you're a liar, a thief, a cheat, unloving or cruel, all in the name of "getting something," you have no wisdom. You will remain lost and never be content with who you are. We have been put on earth to be happy, to grow, to love, to gain wisdom, and none of these things come from money or the relentless pursuit of a career. A sense of purpose comes from feeling fulfilled, being present to ourselves and the people around us, and from celebrating every moment.

When we allow ourselves to fall into the money trap we have moved far away from ourselves. I don't think there's anything wrong with making money and we all need it to live, but it has its place, it needs to be kept in perspective, and it should be made in ways that are satisfying and true to yourself.

In order to reconnect with your true self and what is truly important, I have created the following exercise. It can help you begin to define your true life purpose and move beyond physical attachments.

KNOW THYSELF: MEDITATION TO CLARIFY YOUR VALUES, DREAMS, AND BELIEFS

In order to move forward in discovering and realizing your life purpose you need to examine some old beliefs that may be blocking you. Oftentimes, on a subconscious level, we don't want to know our life purpose because it means we have to make changes our ego isn't willing to make. The life purpose of our true self can be a huge threat to our ego. To know yourself and begin to define what you truly value and what success truly means to you, sit in a quiet place with a notebook, and ponder the following questions:

- What do you think is currently missing in your life?

- What are your current circumstances? Where are you in your life right now? What about those current circumstances may be preventing you from knowing and realizing your life purpose? What would need to change for you to move forward toward knowing your life purpose? (This can be anything from "waiting for my children to grow up," "lack of money," "my parents/spouse/children wouldn't understand or would disapprove," "I must keep my job to pay the mortgage," etc.)

- I want you to identify your values but I want you to list two columns. The first should be The Values of the Ego; the second should be The Values of My Soul. This is not a religious exercise, don't get values and morals confused with each other. A value is something that is important to you. Don't think about it, just write what comes to mind. Afterward, look at the two lists. What is different about the lists; what is the same? Do any of the values overlap? Do any directly contradict or oppose one another?

- Now make a list of your dreams. What has always been your dream life? What would make you happy; what unfulfilled mission is still hiding in your heart? It may seem like a fantasy to you but write it down anyway, let your imagination take over.

• Now look at your values, both sides of the list, and ask yourself where they came from. Did these values come from your parents? From society? How many of them are truly yours? Now look at your dreams. Do your values and your dreams go together? Do some of the values get in the way of your dreams or do they help move them forward? What compromises would you be willing to establish to make your dreams become reality?

• What beliefs do you hold about your dreams that make you feel they aren't valid in some way? Are other people's values getting in the way of you pursuing your dreams? Are you holding onto a belief that tells you you don't deserve your dreams or that they aren't realistic or possible? What if they were possible? What would it take to make them possible?

If you are comfortable in your present life situation, as unsatisfying as it may be, what would motivate you to give up the comfort to pursue your dreams? Leaving the comfort zone, even if it's a painful one, is tough for a lot of people. It can be difficult to leave what you know for what you don't know. Knowing what you really value and what inspires you enough to take risks is a huge threat to the ego. The ego doesn't want to evolve, but the soul must in order to be fulfilled. The ego will fight like mad to prevent your true self from winning. It will say things like, "I'm comfortable, I have enough money, so why give it all up?" or "I have to put my kids through school; I can't quit my job and go back to school" or "If I do X everyone will think I'm crazy; my parents/spouse/children will be upset."

These questions are something you may have to ponder again and again. It isn't a puzzle with one answer; the only answers lie within you. If you begin to examine your values, dreams, and beliefs in the context of who you think you are and where you are in your life, you may begin to see a shift. With a shift in beliefs that may be holding you back, or values that no longer serve you, you can begin to see that you can accomplish what you set out to do. Once you align the values of your soul, your beliefs, and your dreams, everything in the universe will work to turn your dreams into reality sooner than you can imagine.

Creating Your Own Circumstances

Another theme I see again and again comes from clients who feel they are victims of circumstance, blaming everything around them for their problems, when, in fact, they are allowing themselves to be victimized by their own thought processes. We end up hating our work, our environment, the people around us, blaming our boss when we're unhappy with our work or when we aren't "getting ahead."

Technology exacerbates our feelings of disconnect by allowing the world around us to move at such a rapid pace that we have no time for reflection to explore what we might really want to be doing. Maybe your true purpose is to be a painter, but in today's technologically-savvy world you may never find out because when you're young and say, "I want to be a painter" who is going to support that? It simply isn't valued. Oftentimes we make choices about how we live our lives based on the values of others, rather than our own.

One of the strongest points I want to make in this book, and one I constantly try to tell my clients, is that we are not victims of circumstance and we can not allow ourselves to feel victimized by others or our own

weaknesses and lack of perception. No one is a victim of
environment, fate, or destiny. I've already shown you
that there really is no such thing as fate, and if we resolve our karma we can overcome family karma and
growing up in bad environments.

For example, Jack, a well-known television morning
show host, came to see me to hear about his professional future. I sensed immediately that he was on the
verge of a crisis or an opportunity, depending on how
he handled it. I told him he had no future at his current
job, that a new future was about to unfold. "That's not
possible," he roared. "I'm up for a big promotion in
June; they just gave me a corner office." When his con-
tract wasn't renewed, he fell into a deep depression; he
thought he would never work again at his age. He even
considered suicide. This was a man that thousands of
people had seen on television every morning, who was
terrific at his work, and who found a lot of satisfaction
from it. But he hadn't listened to what I told him.

I stayed in touch with him through this time and
had him practice the Karmic Resolution Method. As he
went deeper into it, he gradually began to reconnect
with his self-worth, his positive energy. He was able to
go back to a quiet place in time when the job was not
everything. He realized he had been neglecting his family and his spirit. He began to cheer up; he became more
focused; he realized the job did not define him. He examined the parts of his work that he loved and the parts
where he felt his own values had been compromised. He
knew he had to work from his heart next time, and not
get so wrapped up in the rat race that he neglected his
spirit or his family again.

Letting go of bad karma is a wonderful thing, and

within three months he had a new job where he was able to focus on the things he enjoyed. He was better paid, had more time for his personal life, and his show even won a Grammy Award the following year. When you live from a place that reflects who you truly are, the energy of the universe will come together to help you.

Too often when bad things happen to us we respond by saying, "Oh, it's my fate; I wasn't born under a lucky star" and then we become trapped in a downward spiral. It takes courage and risk to overcome what we think of as our circumstances; it takes insight to become truly powerful; it takes self-knowledge and self-esteem to put yourself on top of the pyramid. I say, if you want something to happen, if you want something to change, say you're going to do it no matter what and then do it.

I've always tried to make things happen in my own life. I was never afraid of difficult experiences or the unknown, such as moving to a new country, changing my culture, learning new languages, expanding my understanding, and changing my path. Because of this I feel like I am living my dreams and I know that I have more dreams yet to live. Thinking this way is a result of having broadened perception, but this type of perception can be created in anyone at any time in their life.

For example, my dear friend Elisabeth was fifty-one years old and had never been a mother. She had always wanted a daughter but all throughout her adult life she never felt like she had the right circumstances for having and raising a child. She was too busy with her career when she was married, and right around the time she felt ready, she ended up divorced. Then she felt she needed to find another man to marry to be the father of her child, but by the time she did, so much time had gone by, she felt she was too old. She didn't think she was physically capable of having a baby and her doctors agreed. Still, she felt at the core of her being that she wanted to be a mother.

She and I started to work together in different ways to accomplish her goal. Her first problem was that she didn't know how to relax and I truly believe that if you are stressed out it's going to prevent you from conceiving. The second thing we did was eliminate the negative emotions she had about being too old. She had to change her belief system, even though everyone else around her held that same opinion. Until she truly believed at her core that she could have a baby at her age, she wouldn't. She had to think it was possible. Finally, we had to unblock her energy, clear her old karma in order to recharge her batteries for such a huge event.

At fifty-two, Elisabeth had a baby girl and she couldn't be happier. Is she tired? Yes, but she told me, "Carmen, I feel so blessed. I'm thanking God every day!" A lot of women like her who are trying to have babies have come to me and I use her as an example of faith, courage, perseverance, and love. I even send some of my clients to talk to her for inspiration. Everything is possible, if there is no fear or denial blocking you, even having a baby at fifty-two years of age.

Underlying every person's life purpose is unconditional love. Our purpose is to give love unconditionally into some area of our life. With Elisabeth it was her mission to give unconditional love to a child. Each person has something to offer that stems from this place of unconditional love. You know you are coming from this place when you are doing something and lose track of time and almost feel that it isn't you who is doing the "doing," you feel like your work is divinely inspired and carried out.

Often to have this type of experience we need to work from our natural gifts and talents. Everyone has them but they aren't always recognized or nurtured. Natural gifts and talents are things that come to you readily, that flow easily from you, that often you take for granted. Perhaps it is a specific ability, like being good with numbers, or writing songs, or dancing, or decorating, or cooking, or having athletic abilities. It may be a certain way with people, a warmth you exude that makes other people feel taken care of; perhaps it is a natural generosity. When you use this gift, you feel at peace, you feel happy, and it comes from your true self.

These gifts are a natural part of who we are and no "circumstance" can take that away from us. The important thing is being aware of what your gifts are and then using them, even if no one has ever nurtured or encouraged these gifts. I want you to learn to encourage and nurture yourself. Too often the things that we take for granted, that we think are easy, may be extremely difficult for someone else. You may think teaching someone to read is easy and so you never see it as a gift. You might think, "Well everyone can teach someone else to read." Not true! You need to recognize that the things you like to do, that you think are "easy" are actually your gifts. Use them.

To help you nurture your natural gifts and talents and use them to overcome "circumstances," I offer the following thoughts.

Discover the Wisdom Within: Trusting Yourself More Than Your Circumstance

Within each of us are many gifts, powers, and unrevealed forces waiting to be unleashed. Often it is unresolved karma that is preventing us from using them. Although "circumstances" can seem to get in the way, only through self-knowledge and trust in our own power can we gain a true sense of self-worth to follow our dreams.

1. Whether you realize it, you are extremely powerful. Acknowledge your own power. This is the force that shapes your life.
2. Identify your skills, your gifts, and your abilities. Think about things you liked to do and were good at even as a child, whether or not you were encouraged to continue to pursue them. You may have to go way back into your memory. What activities do you enjoy, that give you so much pleasure you lose track of time when you're doing them? What skill or ability does this activity require? Make a list of everything.
3. Look at your list—are you using each of these gifts at your highest potential? If not, what is stopping you?
4. In order to unleash your power to create, you must let go of any fear that may be blocking you. What fears do you have about your own power and gifts?
5. Think about how your power and gifts could change your life. Change your vocabulary from "I can't do it" or "Circumstances won't allow me to do it" to "I will do it. It is within my reach."
6. Decide what it is you really want from your life, what is missing, and think of how your power and your gifts can help you.
7. Decide to treat yourself better, give yourself more

> power, more energy every day. Don't let things
> that don't use your gifts or that drain your energy
> get in your way. Eliminate them.
>
> 8. Concentrate your entire mind on your goal and
> be aware that your mind has a much stronger
> capacity than you may believe. The mind is the
> builder, the creator; you are what you decide to
> be. Decide to be proud of yourself by using your
> divinely given gifts. You will astound yourself with
> what you can do.

Project Far

I always say, "Project far." Growing up in Romania, I
knew as a little girl that I wanted to be a famous singer,
that I would travel around the world, be on television.
My family and neighbors all laughed at me. It wasn't
just my grandfather's guidance, or my psychic gift that
allowed me to believe these things, although my broadened perception did allow me to have a vision beyond
what appeared to be an obscure small-town existence.
When the old woman in the wheelchair told me, "You
have gold in your voice," I had no idea what she meant.
But as I got older and my desire to sing got stronger, I
began to pay attention to her message and to use it to
guide me. I projected her prophecy onto my future. So
even though no one believed that I would leave my
hometown and become a singer, I said to myself, "I
don't care; I'm not afraid; I'm going to go as far as I have
to go" and I practiced every day and I entered those
contests and sang my heart out.

When I moved to New York and predicted that my
uncle's patient's husband was going to have a heart at-

tack, she told me, "You must do this work, you must help people." My psychic work was also a calling that I hadn't completely acknowledged and although I didn't know anyone in New York other than my husband and my uncle, people started coming to me. Within a couple of years I was counseling famous actors, singers, Hollywood celebrities, well-known politicians, European royalty, high-powered executives, and members of the medical community. As a little girl in Romania I never would have thought I'd be living in America counseling all of these people, yet I listened to my inner voice and that is where it led me.

People have all kinds of fears, fears of their own power and abilities. I see so many fears even in the richest, most accomplished, brilliant and beautiful people in the world. About eleven years ago, a young actress came to see me and I worked with her for about eight months. I kept telling her, "Pack your bags and go to California; you're going to be very successful there." It took her a long time for her to believe what I was telling her. She had a boyfriend, an older man, and she didn't want to leave him. She was very confused about whether she would succeed. She had no confidence; the timing was off. I made her promise me she would break up with her boyfriend, go to California and give it a chance, and finally she did. She's now a famous actress on one of television's most popular and longest running shows. And she is happily married. I see her now and I'm so proud of her. She didn't believe it could happen, but she took the chance and did it. It would have been easier for her to think small, to play it safe, but then her dreams of being a working actress with terrific opportunities never would have been realized.

Projecting our dreams into reality has a lot to do with timing. Sometimes the timing isn't right to do something. If you truly can't recognize an opportunity, or if something seems too far-fetched, the timing may be off. If we devote time to learning about ourselves and know where we are karmically we will recognize when certain information is coming into our lives. It's all about when certain information comes at a particular time in your life. If you're not ready for it, then you will never succeed. If you're not ready for marriage when someone comes along, then the marriage won't happen; if you don't know yourself and where you are then how can you know what you want from and can love in another person? If you don't know what you want to do with your life then how will you know to seize an opportunity when it shows up?

Often we just can't imagine that something so big might happen to us. I once told a well-known actress that she would win an Emmy award and she didn't believe me. She did end up winning the award a couple of years later. Another woman came to me, a criminal attorney, and I told her, "You're going to meet Hillary Clinton and work for her. You'll eat at the same table as the president." She laughed at me and said, "I don't even know Hillary Clinton, but if I ever meet her, I'll bring her to meet you." Three years later she introduced me to Hillary. She met her through somebody else and started working on her Senate campaign in New York. She became part of the Clintons' inner circle and ate with them more than once.

Seven years ago I told a forty-seven-year-old woman that she was going to be a singer and cut an album. This woman had been seeing me for some time and always felt lost. She came from family money and never had to work, but she never knew, even at forty-seven, what she should do with her life. She didn't feel that she had a purpose. It never occurred to her to sing and she laughed at me and said, "I haven't sung since I was a little girl, Carmen. That's the most ridiculous thing. You're sweet but that's impossible." Three years later she came back to see me and brought her album. She had met a man in the record business six months after she saw me and he had made her an offer. Even though she hadn't sung in so many years, she had a beautiful voice and natural talent and singing made her happy.

We are all here to accomplish something, to bring good energy into the world by our presence. Identifying the good inside of you that can make you flourish and fly is what's important. Once you've recognized your values, talents, gifts, passions, and dreams you will want to develop and share them. You will only feel fulfilled when you do. To guide you toward this I have created the following.

MASTERING YOUR DESTINY: MEDITATION FOR PROJECTING YOUR GOALS INTO THE FUTURE

The only way that you will get what you want in life is to know what you want. And knowing what you want comes from self-knowledge through contemplation and time devoted to your spirit. It comes from paying attention, going through life with your eyes open, awake, and aware. Not letting distractions and ego concerns block you from true self-understanding and a true sense of your own self-worth.

It is possible to make predictions about where your

life is going by projecting your goals onto the future. The more specific you are about your projections, the more accurate your own predictions will be.

There's a technique that has been around for a long time for creating your own destiny that I absolutely believe works. Oftentimes when I work with a client and see an image, by saying what I see out loud, I am projecting their future for them. This technique is a way for you to project your own images into the future. Through the power of the mind you can create your own reality.

This exercise shows how you can transform your own consciousness and project your own future through the power of the imagination. If you can imagine your dream and live as if it were reality, you will find that the universe lines up events until that dream *is* reality.

Take a pen and paper or notebook and sit in a quiet place, away from noise and distraction. Allow yourself to be relaxed and for your mind to let go of any extraneous thoughts.

Now ask yourself what it is you wish for yourself in the future, more than anything else at this moment. It can be a certain career, or being in a relationship, or having children, or living in your dream house, or being free of an addiction or debt. Only you know what you would like your future to be.

Perhaps the image you have for your future is to be able to live in your dream house, on the beach, with your spouse and children with you. Create a vision of what this life would be like in your mind and then pick up the pen and paper and write down the following:

Describe the dream house and its location in as much detail as possible. Where is it? How much land is it on? How is the landscape? How many stories is the house?

How many bedrooms? How many bathrooms? What is the color of the house? How is it furnished? Now describe the house on paper in the present tense, as if it already existed. For example, "I live in a beautiful, yellow, two-story wooden house on one acre of land just a few thousand feet from the Pacific Ocean. There's a wooden pathway that leads through the dunes right down to the water and an Adirondack chair sits at the end of the pathway, where I sit and read a book every afternoon." Continue with that type of description and then imagine the other factors involved. For example, "My two children are with me in the afternoons and build sand castles while I read." Describe the scene in as much detail as you can—this is your image of the future so write whatever you want and be as specific as you possibly can. Remember, it's important to be as precise as you can be in describing detail.

Date this journal entry and then close the journal. Keep this image in your mind but go on with your life as it was. You will find, to your amazement, and long after your conscious mind has forgotten this exercise, that the universe has manifested your image, down to some of the most incredible details.

Our life purpose is to bring good into the world and to be useful—to contribute to the world in some way by our presence. The way that we do this is by identifying the good that is inside of us and making sure that we use it. Identifying our good and using it will require that we grow. Ultimately, whether you're a doctor, a lawyer, an Indian chief, an artist, or a parent, your truest life purpose is for your soul to grow. You can live without a cent in your wallet if you are living from a place of soul purpose. You can be happy if you look at the world from a place of hope. It is my expectation that this book will encourage, awaken, and increase perception and inspire hope in you so that you, too, can find your soul mission and fulfill it.

Remember, it's not how long you live or how much you accumulate, but your spiritual legacy, what you bring to life, that is important.

Now that you've examined how you create and begin to resolve your own karma in connection to your relationships, your well-being, and your life purpose, you have a better idea of what is getting in your way in life, where your problems may be coming from. Your perception has begun to broaden and you're ready to move into the Karmic Resolution Method in the next section.

PART III

HEALING YOUR KARMA:
THE WORLD OF
EVERYDAY ACTION

CHAPTER EIGHT

The Karmic Resolution Method

I first developed the Karmic Resolution Method as a program for my clients to practice in between sessions with me, as a way for them to learn how to access their own wisdom beyond what they learned through our time together. Although I can guide people in the right direction, ultimately the insights and changes that have the most long-lasting impact are those they learn and implement on their own by reaching deeper levels of self-awareness. Every person has his own inner wisdom and the Karmic Resolution Method will help access it.

This Method is a spiritual practice that will help you achieve that level of awareness, help you begin to resolve your karma, and project into reality the life you truly want. Although the Method may take longer in the beginning, as you learn the different steps, eventually you should be able to practice it every day from memory. It will have a remarkable effect on your peace of mind, your stress levels, your ability to solve your problems, to turn your dreams into reality, and become more focused, more loving, and more joyous.

For best results practice my Karmic Resolution Method every night before you go to bed, or every morning when you first wake up. Whenever you decide to do it, make it an automatic part of your daily routine, like brushing your teeth or taking your vitamins. If you do it at night, it will give you a chance to review the events of the day; if you do it in the morning it will help prepare you for the day ahead.

Most important, find a place where you won't be troubled by disturbances from the outside world, including televisions, computers, other people, pets, or loud noises. Create a sanctuary within your environment and within yourself. Being alone inside this "safe place" is perhaps the most valuable way to spend time; it is the first step in discovering who you are.

Sit in a comfortable chair or on a cushion on the floor so that you can be completely relaxed and still. Your eyes should be closed, your hands apart, facing upward. This classic pose will help boost your energy by allowing the energy of the universe to flow through you. Relaxing is not easy and you must be relaxed to apply the Method. First, relax your muscles by concentrating your attention on every muscle from your head, down through your fingers, and then down to your toes. Relax everything, even your facial muscles. Your muscles hold on to tension and stressful thoughts; when you relax them you release the tension.

The first few times you sit down to go through these exercises it could take a half hour or longer. As it becomes more of a regular practice you should be able to go through it in as little as ten minutes a day. Although it may not seem like a lot of time, reflecting consciously on karmic issues for only ten minutes each day will have a tremendous impact on your subconscious mind. Over time this practice will have a cumulative affect on your thought process and your life. It will help you tap into the other 90 percent of the brain that has been lying dormant all these years.

Read through each of the following sections first and then go back and start with step one. It may take you some time with each step to get the hang of it. Take the time you need to do each step properly and then move on to the next step. You'll see that the final step is to record and track your process in a Karmic Resolution Journal. Have this journal and a pen or pencil with you to write down thoughts and memories as they come up.

Step One: Deep Breathing Preparations

It is a good idea to begin any process of introspection with deep breathing which will relax and center you, allowing you to be open to the messages you are about to receive. Think of deep breathing as setting the stage for what is about to unfold.

Deep breathing increases the blood's oxygen level; it counteracts fear and anxiety; it helps eliminate pain. It also strengthens the diaphragm and the solar plexus, the major points of energy in the body. It allows you to start receiving messages from the subconscious mind into your conscious mind. The messages may come in the form of sounds, images, feelings, or ideas. You don't need to do anything with these messages at this point, just be open and accept them.

Breath is a powerful tool and one we don't use in the West nearly enough. Breath not only gives life, it also creates a bridge between the subconscious and conscious mind and connects the mind and the body. When you sit and breathe deeply your physiology will change, and both your mind and your body will relax and become open. Breathing helps clear your head of the thoughts of the emotions and ego, and it allows you to get closer to your true self, your spiritual code. Breathing quiets the mind, allowing us to step away from the events and emotions that may be overwhelming us.

DUAL ENERGY POINTS BREATHING EXERCISE

This exercise is an effective way to create relaxation, calm, focus, and a strong connection between mind and body. It also stimulates two of the most powerful energy points in the body, the diaphragm—your "gut"—and the solar plexus, your central life force.

To do this simple exercise, inhale through the nose, with the mouth closed and exhale through the open mouth. Begin with "gut breathing," bringing oxygen and energy into the home of your instinct, your intuition. Put your hand on your lower stomach, your gut or di-aphragm, and feel how it moves in and out with each breath. On the inhale your stomach will go out as it fills with air, on the exhale it will pull in as the air leaves the body. Take five deep series of inhales and exhales through the diaphragm. Breathe deeply, and pay close attention to each breath, inhale, exhale, inhale, exhale, and the move-ment of your diaphragm in, out, in, out. Take your time.

After five complete breaths move your hand up to your solar plexus, in the center of your rib cage. The solar plexus is the center of your life force and by stimu-lating it with oxygen you create a strong interaction be-tween you and the Invisible World. As you inhale feel your rib cage and chest rise as your lungs fill with air and lower as the air is released. Take five deep inhales and five deep exhales. Take your time and focus on nothing but the act of breathing.

You can repeat this series of five long gut breaths and five solar plexus breaths as long as you need to feel deeply relaxed and connected to your true self. As you breathe in imagine that you are pulling in all the healing energy of the universe, and as you exhale imagine you are exhaling all negativity. You are filling your body and mind with the positive energy of the universe, ridding it of the negative, and connecting deeply to your own life force and gut instinct.

Step Two: Memory Meditation

There are many ways to meditate and many meditation traditions that are practiced by different religious, spiritual, and cultural groups around the world. Traditional meditation has been proven to help heal the body, reduce stress levels, create more focus, concentration, and perspective. My Memory Meditation takes a basic meditation practice and expands upon it to help you access your subconscious memory, where all of your karma is stored.

Meditation can be as simple as sitting quietly with your eyes closed and paying attention to your breathing while observing the thoughts and emotions that pass through your mind. It allows you to be detached from your ego and emotions and allows you to connect to your true self, the self of the Invisible World. Simultaneously, it lets you observe your visible self, the self that functions in the physical world. Meditation bridges the two levels of the mind—the subconscious and conscious minds.

Meditation is not as easy as it looks. You may find it difficult to relax and you may be bombarded with surprising thoughts and insights. Meditation can seem like a paradox because it requires concentration yet the most superior form of meditation is a complete absence of thought. Meditation is the internal activity that directs you toward profound thinking. As you begin, you may feel overwhelmed initially, or elated at the epiphanies you experience.

The Memory Meditation is a powerful tool for allowing your conscious mind to access what is at work in your subconscious mind. It gives you the tools to escape the pressure, emotions, distractions, and concerns of the physical world. If you are feeling overwhelmed or overwrought, meditation is like going on a mental vacation for a few minutes and when you come back home you will think more clearly, calmly, and with greater perspective.

MEMORY MEDITATION

Continue to breathe deeply as in the deep breathing preparations. Breathe in and out, and begin to observe the thoughts that pass through your mind. They may be events that happened that day, feelings you experienced, things on your "to do" list. Imagine that the inside of your forehead is a movie screen and when you close your eyes you can observe your thoughts and feelings as they float across the screen. They appear on the screen and then they fade out. Watch them with the detachment you would have watching images on a screen—they are your thoughts and feelings but you are not thinking or feeling them, just observing them. Think of them as advertisements or coming attractions. Allow the screen to go blank for a few minutes and enjoy the empty screen, the darkness, and the anticipation. Watch as the main feature begins. What will it be?

An image or picture will pop into your mind. It may surprise you. This is your subconscious mind at work bringing forward something that needs your attention. The image that appears will be unique to you but is most likely a memory that will reveal a karmic issue that you've been holding on to. This memory has been lurking in your subconscious behind all the distractions your mind creates. This image may be an event or a person or an object that holds some meaning for you. It could be something from the past, even as far back as your childhood or adolescence, or it could be something that happened that day. Observe this image and be fully aware of it. It is trying to tell you something.

Step Three: Expanding Emotional Awareness

During the Memory Meditation you became aware of a karmic issue or conflict that has lodged itself in your subconscious mind. Now your mind has the power to deal with it consciously, to examine it, and resolve it.

When something is lurking in your subconscious it can be dangerous because you never know when it may show up, in what may seem like an inappropriate way. "Inappropriate" emotional responses are those that occur when someone "pushes your buttons." You will react in a heightened way because of a karmic memory or connection that is hidden in your unconscious. Irrational fears and phobias are also a part of this phenomenon. Expanding your awareness allows you to break the cycle of inappropriate emotions.

THREE KEYS TO EMOTIONAL AWARENESS

KEY ONE: IDENTIFY

Bring the image into focus, put it on freeze-frame, watch it, and ask yourself what emotions does this memory bring up? Don't rationalize the image or think about what it means to you, simply be aware of your feelings and give them a name: anger, fear, frustration, sadness, pride, joy, shame, regret, et cetera. It's amazing how often we let our emotions go unidentified and unchecked. It's like having an anonymous guest show up at your house who runs rampant, destroying your things, all the while ignoring you. This is what your emotions are—you experience them intensely, or you try to stifle them (which only backfires) and they wreak havoc. The only way to get them to stop is to call out to them by name, to identify them.

Let's say the image that came to mind was of you making a speech in a high school debate competition. You see yourself at the podium, looking out at the audience with terror on your face, you freeze up, turn, and walk off the stage. You had forgotten all about this incident and, as a matter of fact, you make presentations at work all the time and they go quite smoothly. Why did this memory surface, and what is it trying to tell you? Or perhaps it is the face of an old lover, someone you haven't thought about consciously for several years.

The primary emotion you may be feeling in regard to the debate competition is shame, a feeling that you weren't good enough, that you were a phony, that you allowed your nerves to get the best of you. The face of the old lover could bring about sadness, regret, a sense of loss, and even though you got "over him" years ago, and are happily married now, thank you, the emotion is still lodged deep inside your memory.

KEY TWO: INTERPRET

Once you've identified the emotions you feel about the conflict or issue that came up, you can begin to acknowledge the root and examine why this feeling has resurfaced now. Are you in another situation where you are afraid of freezing up, of experiencing that type of shame again? What do you think caused that shame to begin with? Why would the loss of an old love show up in your thoughts right now, on this day? Are you in a relationship where you're afraid of experiencing that type of loss again?

Also realize that the image on your screen could have

been something seemingly innocuous, a small incident that happened that day. It could be something a boss or colleague said to you or impatient words you said to your child. The image is not the point. Look at the emotions behind the image and try to see connections between the emotion and other events in your life at this time. Do you find yourself constantly feeling angry or frustrated? Do you often carry a sense of shame? Is fear lurking in your subconscious and holding you back from taking risks?

KEY THREE: EXPAND

Once you've identified and interpreted the emotion you can put it away forever. The way to do this is to expand beyond the smallness of the emotion, to distance yourself from it, objectify it, and know that you, in your essence, are much greater, much stronger, much better than that emotion. Expand your perception and see the illusion that this emotion has created and decide, quite simply, to let it go.

Try the following meditation. Once you get into the practice of using it, you will find that you can control your emotions, rather than having them control you. And when this emotion comes up again, which it will, you will be in a better position to identify it, interpret it, and move away from it.

UP, UP AND AWAY MEDITATION

Imagine that you are in a hot air balloon, down on the ground. In the basket of the balloon are you and the emotion (shame/anger/fear/sadness) you want to get rid of. The hot air goes into the balloon, making it expand and the balloon begins to rise above the ground. But, the emotion in the basket is weighing it down so it can't get very far. There isn't enough room in this basket for both of you if the balloon is going to fly. Imagine identifying the emotion, interpreting what it means and where it came from, and then throwing it out of the basket. Don't worry, it has a parachute. The basket will get lighter, you will feel less crowded and be able to float high up into the sky. From this vantage point you can look down on the emotion, now far away from you on the ground. It looks kind of silly now, very small from this perspective and not quite as important. You can begin to see your life from this much better view and enjoy the ride!

Step Four: Recognizing and Breaking Negative Patterns

When you understand which emotions are dominating your life and begin to view them objectively, you may recognize recurring patterns. The more you practice the Karmic Resolution Method the easier it will be to see what these patterns look like and how they work.

Often we get stuck in behavioral and emotional habits and continue with them because they are familiar. These habits are something you established long ago, that you were probably not even aware of creating.

At the time, this behavior served a purpose for you, but it has ceased to serve its purpose. This habit, or pattern, over time, has become comfortable to you, despite the fact that it can cause you pain and even hold you back from the happiness you deserve. Moving away from the "security" of these negative patterns requires consciousness and energy.

For example, perhaps you are in your late thirties, you've always wanted to get married, and you've been in one monogamous long-term relationship after another but none of them seem to stick. As a matter of fact, they all last two years and right around the time that the subject of marriage comes up, "something happens" and the relationship breaks up. You can't figure out why this keeps happening! Or maybe you choose the wrong person over and over again. It seems that all of these potential life partners share the same bad traits: They drink too much, or cheat on you.

Maybe you have been trying to improve your health by going on a diet and exercise program. Except that you've started and stopped this same exercise and diet program about eleven times. You can stay on the diet for about six days and then you go on a feeding frenzy! And you wake up at 6 A.M. for three days and go for a run but on day four it's raining and you never make it to the park again. Until the twelfth time you start the program.

Or perhaps you've been meaning to get along better with your mother. You love her and she means well, but every time you get on the phone with her or see her, she says something that irks you and you lose your patience and yell at her. You don't mean to yell at her and she has no idea that what she's doing is annoying you, but somehow, no matter how often you tell yourself you'll stop, and no matter how many therapy sessions you go to, it still happens.

All of these situations are examples of negative patterns in action. Sometimes you are consciously aware of the pattern—when you go off your diet and fitness regimen—and sometimes you are not aware—when running away from a relationship as soon as it becomes too "serious."

The reasons for establishing patterns can be complex, and you may never get to the root of them. But, if you can at least recognize them and interpret what they are telling you through expanded awareness, you can break the grip they have on your life.

BREAKING A NEGATIVE PATTERN VISUALIZATION

Although you need to recognize a pattern in order to break it, you don't always need to know why you've established this pattern. Sometimes the most efficient and long-lasting way to break a pattern is simply to let go of it. Action is sometimes more effective than analysis. Often it is the shock of change we fear more than anything, such as when it's hot outside and you want to jump into the pool but you know at first contact, the water is going to be really cold.

The following is a story that resonates for me and many of my clients to illustrate breaking a negative pattern. You can also make up your own story, if that works better for you.

Imagine that you are in a little canoe, riding down the current of a wide river. The river is rocky and the canoe keeps getting caught on the rocks; it's a bumpy ride and the sky is looking overcast and threatening rain. About a mile straight ahead you see a bolt of lightning. There are several little streams that run off the river that will put you in a different direction, away from the storm, but you don't know where they will lead you. The river you're on is the only way you know how to go.

Finally, it starts to rain, and the current is speeding up, pushing the canoe closer to the storm. You know something has to give. You gather your courage and use your paddle to steer you over to the inlet stream. It isn't easy to fight the current but you use all your energy and find yourself in calmer waters. At first, you're nervous as you don't know where this will lead you. But the water is very calm and the ride smooth. The sun comes out, a butterfly flies by, and there are wildflowers growing on the riverbanks. You relax and start to enjoy the beauty and peace around you. You didn't even realize how difficult a ride you had on the familiar river, but you're happy that you managed to get away from it.

Know that the negative pattern you're currently stuck in is like being on that rocky, stormy river. Know that if you can gather the courage to break away, even though you don't know where that other stream takes you, that you will be more calm, relaxed, and open to experiencing happiness.

Step Five: Restoring Equilibrium

Once you've become aware of a negative pattern and decided to steer clear of it, you need to avoid repeating it by remaining in balance. It is when we are thrown off balance by negativity that we are the most susceptible to slipping into old patterns of thinking and being.

One of the best ways to restore balance in your life is by eliminating negativity on a daily basis through, what I call, creating a mental flip-flop. You can use your conscious mind to reprogram your subconscious mind by using imagery that replaces all negative thoughts and beliefs with positive ones. Once you get into the habit of repelling the negative and replacing it with the positive it will be easier for you to work through problems and move forward with your life.

CREATE A MENTAL FLIP-FLOP

Unless you consciously send a message to the subconscious mind to change the old, negative information stored there, that old information, through habit alone, will be stuck there forever and you will be destined to repeat the same negative thought patterns, which result in negative actions and results, again and again. How awful to think that the unhappiness in your life is the result of a bad habit!

Accept yourself the way you are, don't let negative thoughts and self-criticism drag down your energy and self-esteem. Be patient and accepting with yourself and learn to use positive language with yourself. Pay attention to the way you talk to yourself and do a mental flip-flop, turn around the negative to positive. Every time you hear yourself think, "I can't" turn it around and say, "I can." Every time you think, "I'm not" change the thought around to "I am" and every time you think, "I don't know" turn it around and begin the thought with, "I know."

Every time you experience a negative emotion or begin to act on one, stop, and think to yourself how you can do a mental flip-flop and turn it around. If you are frustrated, flip that frustration around to patience. Every time you are angry, flip that anger into a sense of peace and acceptance; every time you feel selfish, flip that into a genuine concern for others. Every time you feel afraid, flip it around to feeling courageous and invincible. The simple act of being conscious of your negative thoughts as you are thinking them and then flipping them around to the positive is a powerful habit that can change your life. And although it is a simple exercise on the conscious level, on a subconscious level it is broadening your perception.

Think of the karmic issue that came up for you earlier in the Karmic Resolution Method. How can you take that issue and do a mental flip-flop?

Step Six: Designing a Vision for the Future

Now that all negative thoughts and emotions have been cleared from your mind, and the wheels have been put in motion to resolve your negative karma, you can begin to visualize the life of your dreams, a beautiful new way of living in accordance with your purest desires. The following exercise will use the power of your mind to envision the future you want and help turn it into reality.

DESIGN FOR THE FUTURE

Now that your mind is in a pure place, free of the draining and distracting influences of negativity, you can create a picture in your mind of the life that you want. Think about the situation or issue that came up earlier during the Method and imagine how life would be if this issue were resolved. Let your imagination create a clear vision in your mind and linger over all of the details of how things would be. Create a vision that is as realistic as possible; don't make this a fantasy; rather create it as if it were truly happening. Make the image real and live in that vision and experience how it feels.

For example, let's say the issue that came up for you was a feeling of constantly having too much to do, of feeling overwhelmed with work and responsibilities. This has made you feel like you don't have time to do the things you would like to do, as well as making you edgy and easy to irritate. Create a vision in your mind of what life would look like, and how you would feel, if you were no longer overwhelmed and "stressed out." Visualize yourself being calm and relaxed, happy in control of your emotions, doing activities you enjoy. Perhaps you are cooking a meal for your friends and family and instead of feeling like it's work, you can relax and enjoy the pleasure in the experience of preparing food for the people you love. Perhaps you are out riding a bicycle with your child, having fun without worrying about time. Perhaps you are in the office and although the phone keeps ringing and there's a pile of work in your in-box, you just calmly go through the work, enjoying the accomplishment and stimulation it gives you.

Perhaps the issue is that you hate your job and have always dreamed of being in some different profession. Or you've always dreamed of traveling or living in Paris. Perhaps you want to be in a more loving relationship. Perhaps you want to be a better friend, or have more time to spend with your children. Create a picture in your mind of working at this other profession, what your day would be like, how your work environment would look, how you would be dressed, who you would be working with, and how you would feel while doing it. Imagine all of the details and linger over the pleasure you feel while being in this vision. Or see yourself living in Paris. Where would you live? How would you spend your days? Who would your friends be? Envision every detail and gain pleasure in living in this space. See yourself in a new relationship, or even the relationship you're currently in, and how it would be if it were more loving. What types of things would you do together? How would you treat each other? What would it look like to be a better friend? How would you behave? What things would you do for your friends? How would you be more available? The same goes for spending more time with your children. How would things be different than they are now? Picture every detail of how it would be and enjoy it.

Once you believe something is possible and have lived in how it feels, nothing can stop it from happening. Everything you want to accomplish can be translated into reality as long as you have released negative thinking patterns. Tell yourself that you can go beyond your limitations, and acknowledge the power within you.

Step Seven: Gathering Powerful Positive Energy

Now that you have envisioned your ideal reality and can imagine how it would feel to live in it, you can begin to take steps to turn it into truth. In order to create a new reality for yourself you will need to recharge your batteries by tapping into the energy of the Invisible World. By tapping into the miraculous healing power of the Invisible World you will feel energized, motivated, and inspired to resolve your karma and make your dreams real. When your goals are aligned with the energy of the universe everything becomes possible.

BATHING IN THE LIGHT

Begin to breathe deeply and as you get into a rhythm, feel yourself accumulating and absorbing cosmic energy. Shut your eyes and in your mind's eye, in the space behind your forehead, picture tremendous white light covering every part of your being. Imagine first that your entire body is full of this light and picture the aura of white light emanating from and surrounding your physical being. As you continue to breathe, increase the amount of light as it emanates out of you and begins to fill the space around you. Lie down and see yourself bathing in this incredible light, see yourself healed, happy, and free from all burdens. Say to yourself, "I am filling myself with the pure white light of the Invisible World. I am full of the light of peace, joy, and wisdom. I am light, I am love, and my life is an expression of this light and love." Lie and bask in this feeling.

Step Eight: Affirmations for Your New Reality

Now that you've envisioned your new reality and have the energy required to make it happen, you need personal affirmations, specific to your vision, that will reinforce your vision and keep you and the energy of the

Universe focused. Sound therapy, saying or hearing something out loud, is a powerful healing tool. Words are powerful and can break through any lingering negative energy.

I think the best affirmations come from the individual and come from the heart. The words you express should come from deep within.

Make a list of the things you want to achieve and the ways in which you want to increase your sense of well-being. Make a list of all the things you like about yourself and things that you are proud of. Write down some of the dreams you envisioned in "Design for the Future." Write down words that express how good you feel right now while practicing the Karmic Resolution Method. From these thoughts create a list of affirmations that affirm the positive energy and emotions that you are feeling, that reinforce your own ability and motivation to turn your dreams into reality, that reflect the hope you have for the future. Be as specific as you can be. You may write things like: "I am blessed with the healing energy of the universe and am capable of living the life I desire," "I am a loving person capable of being in a mutually satisfying, loving relationship," "I am committed to my own personal growth and the universe supports me as I gain more self-knowledge," "I accept myself as I am, with all of my talents and abilities as well as my flaws, and endeavor to create work that I love." Keep a list of these affirmations and turn back to them whenever you begin to feel any negative energy.

Step Nine: Prayers for
Gratitude and Happiness

Two important ways to seal your future and to celebrate your new life is through giving thanks and accepting the happiness you've created in accordance with the universal life force. It is also important to thank your messengers and acknowledge that you appreciate and value their guidance.

The best way to pray is to pray from the heart. Be sincere and spontaneous and be grateful for all of the insight you've received, for being alive, and for feeling connected to the divinity within you. Express the happiness you are feeling right now and pray for it to continue. The Universe wants you to be happy and fulfilled and to evolve into the best person you can be. Expressing thanks and joy as you travel on this path is key to your own progress and well-being.

Step Ten: Recording and Tracking Your
Progress in a Karma Resolution Journal

Writing things down gives them power. It can also help you to clarify your thoughts and record your progress as you work on different karmic issues. There are many different ways to keep a Karma Resolution Journal and it is up to you as an individual to decide what you want to record.

I find that it's helpful to keep your journal by your side every day as you go through each step of this Method. As you complete each step record any images, thoughts, or realizations that occur to you. This can

help you focus on specific karmic issues you've identified as you go through each step in the process. For example, you can write your images from the Memory
Meditation, record the emotions you identified and patterns you recognized, write down visualizations for your
new reality, as well as your affirmations and prayers you
created that are specific to that issue. Sometimes resolving karma can be like unraveling a mystery or putting
together a puzzle. Your issues or past karma may not be
immediately apparent and will become clear only over
time. All of the different clues and pieces add up to a
bigger picture of who you are. By keeping the different
clues and pieces in a journal you can eventually see the
big picture clearly.

For this reason I find that it's helpful to go back at the
end of every month and review your progress. This will
encourage you by showing you how much improvement
you've made and may lead to new insights. Sometimes
after a certain issue is revealed to you, the subconscious
mind needs to sit with it for a while before you can begin to resolve it. Having your insights recorded in your
journal help you to pinpoint what you've learned when
the distractions of day-to-day life take you away from
yourself. And sometimes the best insights and resolu-
tions come when you sit quietly and go back over the
journal.

The Karmic Resolution Method may take some dili-
gence and you may need to face issues you've ignored
or suppressed before now, but over time it will help you
develop the self-awareness you need to resolve your
karma and project your own happy future. Good luck!

Prophecies and Predictions for the Time to Come

I have made many predictions over the years, many of them made on television, and I've been known to have 92 to 93 percent accuracy. For example, I made the following predictions, many of them in 1997 and 1998 on *Good Day New York* and the Channel 11 morning news, all before they happened:

- After a lot of confusion Russia would turn into some form of democracy. In 1998, when Yeltsin was sick, I saw a new president with blond hair whose name started with the letter *P* who would enter office in 1999. On the last day of 1999, Vladmir Putin became the new Russian president.

- I said that President Clinton would almost be ousted from office but would stay on as president. He would then disappear into civilian life.
- I said that Al Gore would win the presidency but would not be put in office.
- In 1998, I was on *Good Day New York* and said that Mayor Giuliani would drop out of the senatorial race in May for health reasons and that he'd have legal problems. In May 2000, he dropped out of the race because he had prostate cancer, and he also filed for divorce. I also said that Hillary Clinton would run for office and win (this was in a private reading for the woman who became Hillary's campaign adviser, before there was even talk of her entering politics). She is now New York's senator.
- In January 1998, I predicted that a new planet would appear in our galaxy. In June 1998, *The New York Times* reported that a new planet was noticed in our solar system. This planet is twice the size of Jupiter. I also reported that we would go to Mars and discover water, and in 1999, we did.
- In August 1997, the day after Princess Diana died, I went on TV and said that Mother Teresa would die in a week, and she did. I also said that the next internationally famous person who would die and draw a lot of attention and pub-

lic sympathy was a young man who would die in an airplane in two years. That was JFK Jr.

• I am the first to admit I know nothing about baseball, but I predicted on live television the subway series with the Yankees winning before either team had even made it to the play-offs.

While many of these predictions amazed and surprised people, I've always felt, as I've said many times in this book, that the point of making predictions is to help people prepare and make the appropriate changes to prevent bad things from happening. And while it's interesting and helpful to make predictions on a small scale, the real purpose of my gift is to see patterns, trends, and major changes so I can help guide humanity to evolve spiritually and gain more knowledge about our purpose on earth. Ultimately I am more interested in the "bigger picture" of where humanity is going.

In my work I've seen many people be afraid of predictions or deny them altogether, but they shouldn't scare us and, in the future, as we gain more knowledge and awareness, we will understand how to use predictions to avert negative events.

If we look at the past several centuries of human history and evolution, it is amazing how much life on earth has changed from one century to another. Look at where we were just one hundred years ago, and with the escalation of technology, look at how much has changed in even the past twenty years! It would have been incredible five hundred years ago to imagine how we would be living in this time today. Empires come and go, civilizations try to gain control and conquer the earth, and humans appear and disappear. Through all of this, humanity has evolved and man has made advancements to make their lives better in many ways. But humans never resolved the mysteries of their own existence. Until now.

The world today is at a crossroads. Man is the creation of God, and what we've come to know as God is the perfection of the infinite universe. A shift in the consciousness of humanity is happening as we leave the place of "I believe in God" to the place of "I know God." We will come to evolve spiritually, to know our creator and be in tune with our creator so that our existence is a reflection of this divine perfection, rather than the evil qualities of human nature.

We have entered a different era and will be in transition until 2033. After these years of change and transition, we will enter an era of peace. We will be more aware of our ability to have a direct relationship with God, and the more we enter into a partnership with the universe, the more we apply the force of God within us and outside of us. We will become more aware that the true meaning of life and the way to gain wisdom is to seek and find God. If you live this principle of truth, you will be able to call upon the force of this truth to have health, happiness, and enlightenment. So although we have been living through human laws for thousands of years, we will make the transition to living through universal laws. We will learn how to eliminate the dark and destructive forces during this transitional period, so there is less fear and less confusion in the time to come.

When I talk about this new world, what I mean is that from an astrological point of view we are entering a new time. We are leaving the era of Pisces and entering the age of Solaris (or Aquarius as many people call it), where we will be for the next 2000 years. Astrologically speaking, the era of Solaris—the era of light or the eleventh house—is ruled by the planet Uranus, the "awakener," whose characteristics involve sudden changes. With Uranus as a ruler, changes will take place in the world instantly, unexpectedly. Uranus is the first of the transcendental planets, and its actions are sudden, violent, breaking from the past, breaking from tradition, and bringing in the new. This means new laws, new inventions and discoveries, and new science. It literally means there will be a new world overnight. However, we will not enter this new world until the transition from Pisces to Solaris is complete, probably around 2033.

During this transitional period, humanity will face many challenges. There will be natural disasters, earthquakes, and, of course, the continuing war in the Middle East. Pakistan, Afghanistan, India, and Iraq are a huge concern for the world, and the war that has begun is one of huge proportions. There will be a new leader in the Asian world, someone young and rebellious, who will try to instigate problems between these countries. The war will last for fifteen years as we go through a learning process, and we will need to proceed with care and compassion and diplomacy. The ex-communist countries will also be in big financial trouble in the next five years and will add to the conflict. The pope will die, and Catholicism will face even greater problems than it already is today. The death of the pope will bring a lot of fear and confusion and war and poverty into the world, and eventually Catholicism will change into a different religion. Queen Elizabeth will no longer be queen in four years. Diana's first son, William, will become king for a short time and will then agree that the monarchy is an archaic system that no longer works. England will become a democratic regime, and Europe will be one unity. There will also be tremendous conflict in this country between the democrats and the republicans over the next two years. President Bush needs to be aware that the terrorists want to kill him and that he is in danger for the next one year and eleven months.

This is a lot of conflict and change, but the point of all of it is that our systems are no longer working. They all work through the human laws, which is why there is so much conflict and suffering. As we are faced with change and conflict, we need to change our systems toward the universal laws. The events of September 11, 2001, were a tremendous symbol of this conflict. It happened on the eleventh day of the month; the first airplane to fly into the towers was flight number eleven; the twin towers standing next to one another looked like an eleven; and humanity has recently entered the eleventh house—Aquarius. This is not a coincidence. Our lives will never be the same after this event; it is the beginning of a new life on earth, but there is a long transitional process.

Change and conflict scare people, but this transitional period over the next twenty-seven to thirty-one years is all about creating harmony and connecting to the divine and creating a sense of wholeness, within our bodies, in our relationships, and on our planet. While this is happening, everything will be changing: our monetary system, our health system, our environment, and our politics.

From a technological standpoint, humanity will reach a peak in evolution in the next twenty to thirty years, and we will rapidly move to a better world where we will feel safer. There will still be war in this time, and religious conflicts and karmic issues that have existed for thousands of years will need to be resolved. As a result, however, after all of this conflict, we will come to acknowledge one God in a new religious concept. Religion as we've known it will be eliminated, and there will be one world religion acknowledging one God. All the religions are going to go away, some gradually, which you can already see happening. We'll see God in a different way, and we will all come to this same, new understanding. We will have different places of worship and learn to pray differently. There will be another prophet, something and someone beyond us who will show us this new understanding.

In the next ten to thirty years, the female energy will be much stronger and dominant. This new prophet will be a woman, not a man, and she will start writing books of prophecies. She will be the same age Nostradamus was when he began to write down his prophecies, fifty to fifty-two years old. Humanity will recognize her and will listen.

A woman will also lead America in the near future.

In the next 150 years, we will no longer have politicians or presidents. The monarchy and the papal system will both be demolished. We will become aware that this type of power doesn't belong to any one individual, that the only real power is the collective consciousness, or God.

We will have one monetary system all over the world, and we will no longer have paper money or a stock market. Our monetary system will work with codes. We are no longer going to have financial discrepancies in the world, which is such a huge cause for suffering and violence. There will be enough for everyone. We will eventually live in a time where our accomplishments will not be measured by "money."

The entire medical system will change as we begin to treat the whole person: the hospitals, the health and medical plans, the technologies. We will make medical developments so advanced that we will never cut the body again. We'll stop using the knife and do only laser surgery—light will become our major tool of healing. In the era of golden light, we will be disease free. We will interpret the genetic code and prevent disease from happening. We will also come to acknowledge that a state of health is also the result of a state of content in the mind, and we will come to be much happier people. We will heal the body by healing the aura first. We will put sick people into a tube of energy, not unlike an MRI, and using what we learn from the genetic code, we will go into the tube and be healed. We will also eliminate all the diseases of the blood, such as diabetes, cancer, AIDS, and high blood pressure. And we will find a new way to perform heart surgery.

We will also find ways to slow down the aging process. We will start living 125 to 175 years in the next 50 to 150 years as gravity begins to slow down, keeping us on the earth longer.

In the new belief system that develops we will also come to heal on an emotional level and begin a more harmonious way of living called The Era of a Thousand Years of Peace. The era of guns, of our children killing one another, of drugs and bombs will all come to an end.

In 2007, the earth will be hit by a meteorite as a lesson for us to wake up, but there will be no major tragedies. It won't be a major hit but enough of a threat and scare to shock us into awakening and coming together. We will be aware that we may be in danger from threats beyond ourselves, and we have to stick together. As we come to see the world differently through this frightening event, we will be taking a strong step forward.

Eventually, much further in the future, when our planet is threatened, human beings will survive by leaving earth and moving as a species to another planet in a different galaxy called Iris.

In the meantime, our way of traveling in space will completely change. Our airplanes will look very different in the next twenty-five years, and we will go into space in the next 80 to 128 years. Everyone in the future will have his own airplane, much the way we all have our own cars today.

We will develop computers the size of a watch that will anticipate and know what we need and where we are. They will guide us in working with our natural biorhythms. This same wristwatch-like computer/telephone will have a small screen, and we will wear it on our left hand to communicate with each other.

We will start to use more than 10 percent of the brain. Humanity will eventually be able to communicate telepathically. We will be more aware of our mind's potential and will learn to levitate and use telekinesis. We will also be able to communicate regularly with our loved ones on the other side.

Man will erase evil from the earth within 150 years.

PHOTO: © JOSH GOSFIELD

CARMEN HARRA is a doctor in Clinical
Psychology, Clinical Hypnotherapy and
Alternative Healing (Albert University and
Somerset University). A numerologist,
astrologer, and astrophysionomist, Carmen is a well-known singer and has her
own jewelry line on QVC. She lives in
New York and Hollywood Florida. Visit
her at: www.carmenharra.com.